Blue

Ancient American
Art IN DETAIL

Ancient American
Art IN DETAIL

Colin McEwan

THE BRITISH MUSEUM PRESS

This book is for my parents

HALF-TITLE PAGE: Turquoise mosaic of a double-headed serpent,
Aztec, Mexico, AD 1400–1521 (see pp. 16–17).

FRONTISPIECE: Detail of a double-spout and bridge vessel with
puma deity and trophy head, Nasca, Peru, 2nd century BC–
6th century AD (see p. 127).

RIGHT: Detail of a red bag with double-headed bird motif, Ica, Peru,
10th–15th century AD (see p. 69).

© 2009 The Trustees of the British Museum

Colin McEwan has asserted the right to be identified as the author
of this work

First published in 2009 by The British Museum Press
A division of The British Museum Company Ltd
38 Russell Square, London WC1B 3QQ
www.britishmuseum.org

A catalogue record for this book is available from the British
Library

ISBN 978-0-7141-2582-4

Photography by the British Museum Department of Photography
and Imaging

Designed and typeset in Minion and Helvetica by Peter Ward
Printed in China by C&C Offset Printing Co., Ltd

The papers used in this book are natural, renewable and recyclable
products and the manufacturing processes are expected to conform
to the environmental regulations of the country of origin.

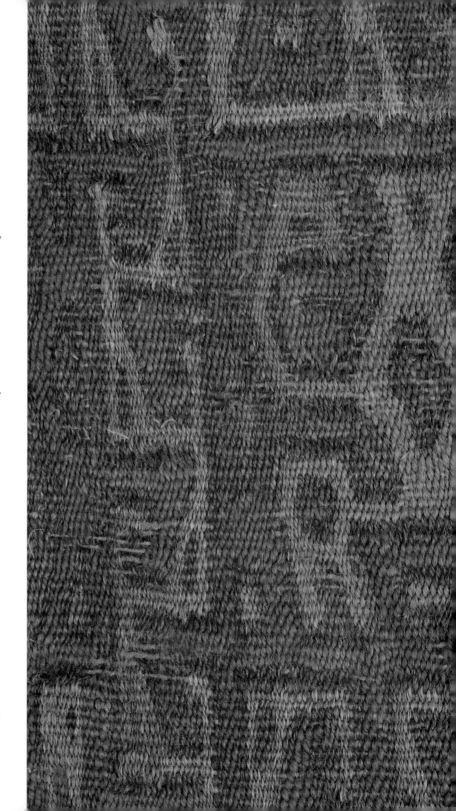

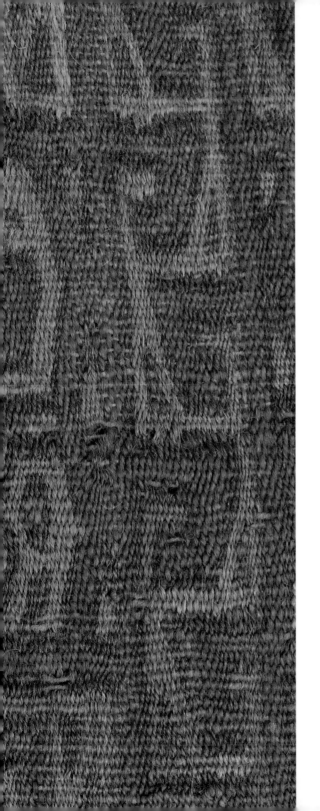

Contents

Preface

All human societies share a need to explain the origins of life, to train children and guide them through puberty towards adulthood, and to teach the roles and responsibilities that underpin community life. They must also assure collective well-being and defence, be led wisely and prepare for death. This book draws on the breadth and depth of the British Museum's American collections to explore these themes through chapters organized around significant stages in the human life cycle. It features masterworks encompassing cultures from Alaska to Patagonia and from prehistoric times up to the early 20th century, juxtaposing works from within as well as between different traditions in order to suggest new comparisons and connections.

Since their inception, museums have played a vital role in bringing 'the arts' of the Americas to the attention of international audiences. Beginning with informal antiquarian interests in the 17th and 18th centuries, collecting practices have long reflected the changing relationships between collectors and collected. The more formal classification and exhibition of 19th-century collections as examples of primitive 'art and industry' tended to emphasize the great gulf between what objects originally meant for their makers and what made them the focus of such intense acquisitive interest to visitors from other cultures.

With the emergence of art history as a new discipline in the late 19th century, the works chosen to illustrate the first art-historical surveys of the Americas were selected primarily for distinctive aesthetic qualities considered typical of pre-Columbian 'art'. Increasing knowledge led to more thorough treatments, grouping together outstanding works from the same regional traditions and incorporating references to settlement plans, architecture and archaeological context. Subsequently there have been profound changes in the way the works of indigenous traditions are viewed, valued and understood. There has also been a critical reappraisal of the Western notion of 'art' and its application to non-Western cultures. Technological and stylistic innovation among traditional societies throughout the Americas stems from a direct engagement with the creative powers of a universe in which 'man' is not considered separate from 'nature'. Amid the creative diversity shaped by particular environmental and social circumstances, an essential strand of cultural continuity is inspired by this very different way of perceiving and experiencing the world.

Readers familiar with this region will recognize many iconic works which are complemented by others seen here for the first time. The focus on individual objects and the insights their details can reveal is intended to encourage references to related objects and themes in other chapters. I hope this approach may stimulate different ways of thinking about objects and open up new perspectives about the various ways in which they acquire meaning and can be interpreted.

I wish to warmly thank Nina Shandloff for her unstinting support, forbearance and wise counsel; Julia Zumstein who has ably managed the myriad details involved in the preparation of the volume; and Harry Persaud, Stewart Watson, Helen Wolfe, Kirsten Halliday, Stewart Marsden and Ian Taylor for their practical help with object selection and access. I am especially indebted to Ivor Kerslake, John Williams, Dave Agar and Mike Row of the Department of Photography and Imaging for their patience and professionalism. My colleagues Ben Burt, Simon Martin, Jose Oliver, Robert Storrie and George Lau and my partner Norma Rosso have contributed helpful comments and suggestions.

Coiled rattlesnake. Basalt, Aztec, Mexico, AD 1400–1521. Ht 36 cm, diam. 53 cm. This powerful sculpture reveals how closely the rattlesnake's anatomy and habits were observed. Two small holes, one on either side of the snout, house the infrared heat sensors that enable the snake to seek out and strike prey at night. Each year upon shedding its skin it would also grow a new rattle. There are 13 segments on the tail of this specimen – perhaps an allusion to the 13-day period in the Aztec divinatory calendar (*tonalpohualli*). (See pp. 14–17, 95, 96, 124–5.)

1

What is Ancient American Art?

Nomadic hunters, fishermen, farmers and urban dwellers in traditional societies all depend on an intimate knowledge of the landscape, plants and animals to assure their survival. Contemporary indigenous Americans speak of a dynamic, active relationship between the visible material universe and other invisible worlds that are no less real. Powerful spirit beings that are invisible to ordinary consciousness are also capable of assuming material form in different guises.

Many of the works featured in this book illustrate the intense engagement between maker and material, wrestling to transcend the division between visible and invisible domains. They also reveal the ways in which the practiced eyes, tools and techniques of skilled artisans combine to achieve aesthetic mastery – what we conventionally refer to as 'art', although their makers never regarded this as a separate category based on idealized concepts of beauty. We therefore need to rethink how we classify and label 'art' objects and to grasp very different modes of perception, values and experience. This offers the key to understanding ancient American approaches to various materials and to the way that form, function and meaning were inextricably linked.

The relationship between human settlement and the landscape is the undisclosed backdrop to the works presented here and in which they once found full significance for their makers. Earthen platform mounds ranging from formative Olmec sites in Mexico's Gulf coast lowlands to the mound-building cultures of the Mississippi Valley find their counterparts in the adobe pyramids of coastal Peru and the stone temples, tombs and palaces that later rose elsewhere across the Americas.

The texture and colour of quarried stone impart an unmistakable character to the great Pueblo dwellings of the American Southwest, Teotihuacan in highland Mexico, cities in the Maya lowlands such as Tikal, Palenque and Uxmal as well as Chavín de Huantar and Wari in Peru and Tiwanaku in the Bolivian highlands, to name but a few. Many of these sites were the setting for monumental stone sculpture representing revered deities and deified ancestors. Some like Teotihuacan with its spectacular polychrome murals have been described as painted cities and in others such as Tiwanaku there is evidence for

Opposite: **Alabaster vessel with figure of a crouching warrior. Veracruz (Isla de Sacrificios), Mexico, AD 900–1521. Ht 23 cm.** This vessel was probably a revered personal possession invested with the power and prestige of its owner – perhaps the skilfully sculpted warrior himself. It was taken as an offering during a long-distance pilgrimage to the island sanctuary of Sacrificios, just south of Veracruz, where a cult to Quetzalcoatl was celebrated in pre-Columbian times.

sheets of hammered gold adorning wall facades.

In due course emerging imperial designs began to shape the world anew. The conversion of the lake marshes around the Aztec island capital of Tenochtitlan in the Mexican highlands into a highly ordered productive agricultural landscape of floating gardens was matched in South America by the Incas' transformation of the vertiginous mountain slopes of the Andes into the irrigation canals and elegant sweeps of tiered terraces that flank the Urubamba Valley.

The major urban centres were instrumental in fostering and diffusing distinctive styles in media ranging from stone and pottery to textiles and in many cases metalwork. The aesthetic sensibility that governed large-scale programmes of public architecture is echoed in a range of portable works in stone carefully selected for its durability, colour, translucence and graining. Wood was among the earliest natural materials used for domestic dwellings, tools and weapons. In the Caribbean, before fashioning sculptured anthropomorphic and zoomorphic figures from durable tropical hardwood, Taíno shamans first addressed the spirit being in the tree to determine what form it wanted to assume. The towering trunks of native conifers on Canada's Northwest coast were used to sculpt images of the founding animal ancestors of clans and

lineages while asserting ties to the resources of rivers, land and sea.

The malleable, tactile qualities of clay made it a natural medium for creating not only utilitarian wares but also modelled figurines, portrait vessels and symbolic forms. The growing mastery of firing technology and range of colours advanced hand in hand with stylistic development, and Moche and Nasca vessels were effectively deployed as a canvas for applying a 'painted codex on pottery'. In addition to stone and pottery, writing and painting were applied on perishable bark, deerskin and other forms of recording to represent oral traditions, births and deaths of rulers and dynastic genealogies, battles and other important events.

Prior to European contact, the availability of written sources that could inform us about indigenous religious systems and rulership are limited to Mesoamerica – none were invented in either North or South America. Nor are there references to named artisans. Instead, we have first-hand accounts from members of traditional communities, sometimes supplemented by records from the early colonial period. Both help with the challenge of describing, interpreting and understanding these richly expressive works in ways that are faithful to their original meaning and significance.

2

The Origins of Life

Creation stories recounted down the generations among different traditions tell how the world came into existence, the sky became separated from the earth and the alternation of night and day was established. They describe how the gods fashioned the first humans and how diverse creatures assumed their forms and habits. In the Andes, for example, unusual geological formations are read as evidence of ancestral events and as landmarks left by the deeds of mythological figures. Caves, lakes, springs, rock outcrops and prominent peaks are all key elements in an animate landscape inhabited by powerful deities. Similarly, in the vast reaches of the Amazon Basin, inscribed or painted motifs on the bedrock and boulders adjacent to waterfalls and rapids mark the presence and deeds of founding ancestors in times past. In common with rock art traditions across the Americas, these signs play a vital role in naming and incorporating such places within an ordered cultural universe. Ancestral ties to the land also reinforce territorial claims by friend and foe and are instrumental in asserting collective identity.

Close attention was paid to the celestial and subterranean realms. The daily path of the sun and moon and their annual journeys along the horizon determined the cyclical rhythms that governed all forms of earthly life. Their waxing and waning followed seasonal and monthly cycles that were complemented by the rising and setting of constellations such as the Pleiades that heralded the beginning of the agricultural year in many cultures. The waters of the ocean concealed a dark underworld that was the source of primordial forms of life as well as nourishment including shellfish, crustaceans and abundant shoals of fish. Humans competed with sea lions for subsistence resources along with fearsome predators such as the killer whale that figures so prominently in the imagery of Pacific coastal cultures. Rivers fed from distant sources were essential to terrestrial life, supplying water that mediated the rhythms of the cosmos into the forces of plant growth. The sinuous movement of snakes was often likened to the curving meanders of flowing streams and serpentine motifs were used as a metaphor for water itself. Snakes' habit of annually shedding their skin led to an association with regeneration and renewal. Mysterious metamorphoses could be observed

Aztec origins in Aztlán, Codex Aubin. Watercolour on paper. Aztec-Colonial, Mexico, *c*. AD 1576–96. Ht 15.5 cm, w. 13.4 cm (each sheet).
Aztec groups trace their origins to an ancestral homeland known as Aztlán. In this scene Aztlán is depicted as an 'archetypal' island in a watery expanse with four 'house' glyphs marking the cardinal directions. The location has been variously interpreted as a distant island in the Pacific off the west coast of Mexico or perhaps the island setting of the Aztec capital Tenochtitlan itself in Lake Texcoco. Throughout the Americas oral traditions use different kinds of images, scenes and objects to represent mythical origins (see pp. 24–5).

in freshwater lakes and ponds as tadpoles turned into frogs. At the mouths of estuaries where rivers merge into the sea, wetland marshes hosted a profusion of bird life. In desert regions too, plants, birds and animals inspired the painted scenes and designs for pottery traditions from the arid American Southwest to the coast of Peru (see ch. 5).

Certain animals were accorded particular significance. Powerful nocturnal hunters including crocodilians, jaguars and pumas are complemented by aerial raptors such as eagles and hawks that feature in the imagery on temple facades guarding access to carefully controlled sacred spaces. The ability of some species of snakes to move freely between water, earth and the forest canopy enhanced their symbolic role as intermediaries between the different layers of the cosmos: underworld, earth and sky. All these, together with a range of other creatures with composite attributes, pervade the religious iconographies of the Americas.

Human health and fertility were supremely important to the future well-being of society. Men and women played vital and complementary roles in assuring the reproductive capacity of the community, calling upon the virile potency of revered ancestor figures. With growing populations increasingly dependent on agriculture, it is not surprising that the pantheon of creator deities was closely linked with powerful environmental forces – sun, thunder and lightning, wind and rain. These cosmic agents formed the focus of cults and shrines as well as objects wrought in materials ranging from jadeite and turquoise to gold and featherwork. Connections were effected by costumed priests who participated in the pageantry of processions and ritual re-enactments accompanied by the rhythmic cadences of chant and dance.

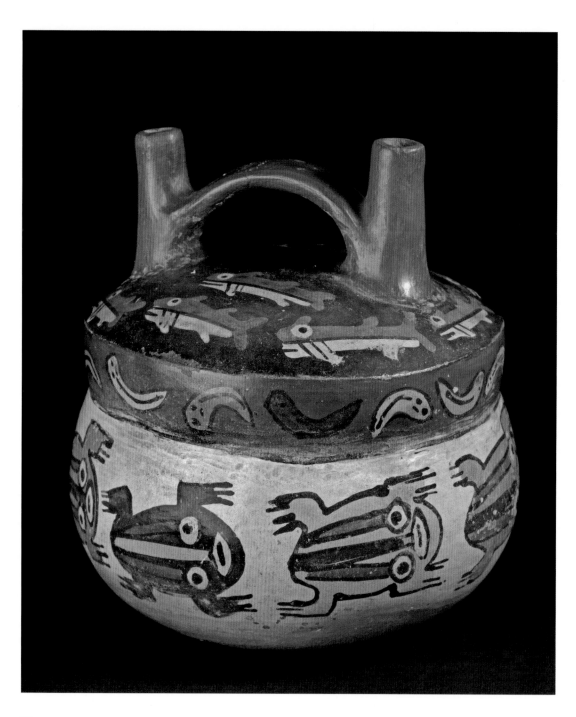

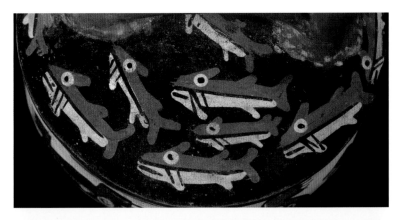

Double-spout and bridge ceramic jar.
Nasca, Peru, 2nd century BC–6th century AD.
Ht 18 cm, diam. 16.5 cm.

Nasca people depended for subsistence on an array of domestic crops grown in narrow, fertile river valleys, combined with the rich marine resources of the coastal littoral and deep-sea fishing. Three superimposed bands of repeated motifs encircle this vessel featuring creatures that inhabit the watery realm. On top a row of fish is painted on a black background that may equate with the dark underwater world, night and primordial time. A central band contains tadpoles and beneath this is a row of frogs. When the vessel is inverted to discharge the liquid the hierarchy is reversed, matching more closely the order observable in the natural world – the sea creatures of the ocean are on the bottom, while in the middle are the tadpoles that will eventually metamorphose into amphibious frogs that can venture on to the upper terrestrial world.

Playing with such inversions is apparent elsewhere in Nasca iconography in which the visual logic communicates fundamental contrasts between day and night and between wet and dry seasons. These rhythms shape the hunting and feeding patterns of different creatures as well as their breeding and migratory habits. All were integrated into the closely observed ecological cosmology portrayed in Nasca art (see pp. 124–5, 127).

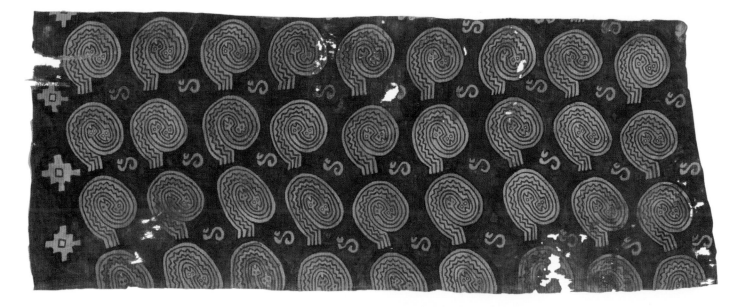

Textile with snake motifs.
Painted cotton. Chimú, Peru, 11th–12th century AD.
Ht 64.5 cm, w. 164 cm.

Textiles and pottery from Peru's Pacific coast are frequently painted in muted hues that echo the austere palette of the desert landscape. Here, life depends on the annual replenishment of the rivers fed by meltwater and rain from their sources in the high Andes, and the swelling torrent filling a dry stream bed is sometimes likened to the body of the *amaru* – a feared semi-mythical snake-dragon that periodically descends from the mountains. The principal motif of a coiled pair of snakes is repeated in uniform rows. Each motif culminates in a central pair of opposed snake heads that might be read as an expression of the complementary oppositions that governed aspects of native Andean cosmology and social organization. The 'stepped cross' or *chakana* symbol appears on the left-hand side and is widely used in American cultures to signal sacred central places serving as a portal into the underworld below or celestial realm above.

Stone ritual vessel (*cocha*) with snake motifs.
Inca, Peru, late 15th century AD. Ht 15 cm, w. 40 cm.

This massive circular ritual vessel or *cocha* (see also pp. 92–3) is
sculpted from a single block of the black volcanic basalt found in the
vicinity of Cusco. It is one of a small number of surviving vessels of
this size that were probably housed in the Coricancha – the Temple of
the Sun – or adjacent sacred precincts of the Inca capital. It was likely
used as a receptacle for liquid offerings, perhaps simply to hold water
and create a still, reflective surface regarded as an 'eye' seeing into
the underworld. The tightly nested concentric coils of the snake's body
mimic the whorls and eddies that allude to the dynamics of moving
bodies of water. A total of ten serpent heads are symmetrically arrayed
around the vessel rim, a pattern resembling the radial arrangement of
the *ceque* system used by the Incas to organize space in Cusco, the
imperial capital, and the land beyond, like the slices of a pie.

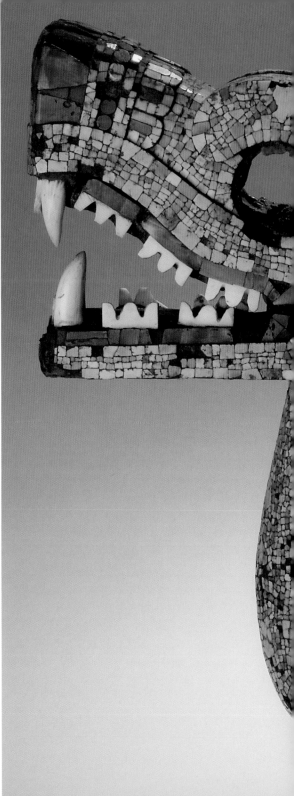

Double-headed serpent.

Turquoise mosaic on wood. Mixtec-Aztec, Mexico, AD 1400–1521.

Ht 20.5 cm, w. 43.5 cm.

This iconic image of a double-headed serpent may represent a 'sky-band' symbolizing the celestial realm. It was an emblem of authority, perhaps once part of an elaborate suite of ritual regalia worn or carried on ceremonial occasions. It is carved in cedar wood (*Cedrela odorata*), which served as a base upon which a skilfully worked pattern of tiny cut and polished turquoise mosaic *tesserae* was applied using pine resin adhesive. Turquoise was highly valued in Mesoamerica and was obtained by Aztec trading emissaries (*pochteca*) from mines in what is now the southwest United States, far beyond the limits of the Aztec empire. The worked tiles were carefully selected and graded by size and colour then laid in to recreate the subtle patterning of the snake's scales. Details around the nose and mouth of both serpent heads are picked out in red thorny oyster shell (*Spondylus princeps)*, conch shell (*Strombus galeatus)* was used for the white teeth, and polished orbs of iron pyrite may once have been placed in the eye sockets. The intense blue-green hues of turquoise evoke associations with Quetzalcoatl ('feathered serpent'), one of the most powerful Aztec deities and culture heroes (see pp. 18–19). Serpentine imagery is also associated with other ancient Mesoamerican divinities, particularly Xiuhcoatl and Tlaloc (see pp. 95–6).

Greenstone bust of Quetzalcoatl.
Aztec, Mexico, AD 1325–1521.
Ht 32.5 cm, w. 23 cm.

Quetzalcoatl – 'feathered serpent' – was one of the principal deities in the Aztec pantheon and inspired a cult throughout Mesoamerica. In his manifestation as Quetzalcoatl – Ehecatl, the God of Wind – he is associated with moisture-laden storm clouds whose powerful gusts bear life-giving rains, hence the choice of the dark green stone for this sculpture. Quetzalcoatl was also a legendary culture hero, said to have emerged amid feathered serpentine coils. The prized iridescent green feathers of the quetzal bird were widely used in costume and adornment to signal verdant sources of moisture and as special symbols of authority.

According to Aztec creation stories, four suns or worlds came into existence before the present one, but each ended in a cataclysm. When the fourth epoch was destroyed by floods, the gods decided to start afresh. To create a new race of humans, Quetzalcoatl descended to the lower levels of the Underworld. He tricked Mictlantecuhtli, the Lord of Death (see pp. 134–5), to retrieve the bones of the people of the fourth sun. With those bones and some of his own blood, he then gave life to the humans who inhabit the present world. Quetzalcoatl was also an arbiter between life and death, shown (far left) by the severed head he holds in his left hand, and the cryptic symbols amid the feathers on his back.

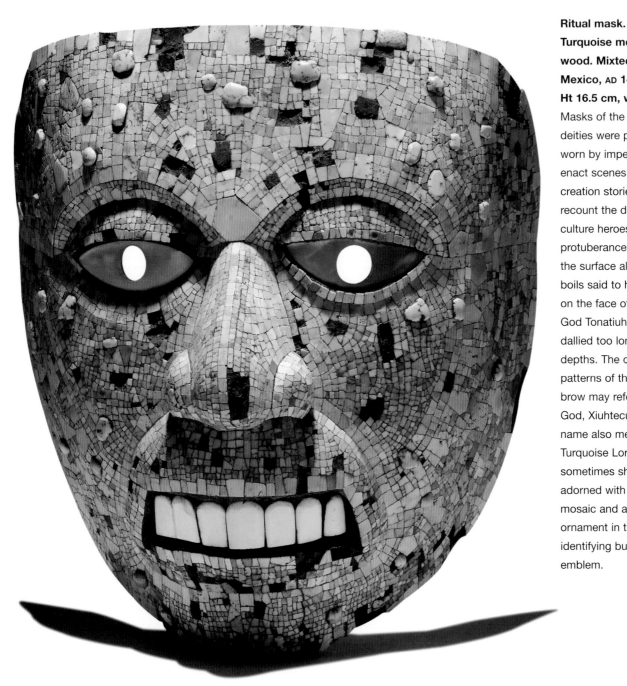

Ritual mask.
Turquoise mosaic on wood. Mixtec-Aztec, Mexico, AD **1400–1521. Ht 16.5 cm, w. 15.2 cm.**
Masks of the major Aztec deities were probably worn by impersonators to enact scenes from creation stories and to recount the deeds of culture heroes. The protuberances visible on the surface allude to the boils said to have erupted on the face of the Sun God Tonatiuh when he dallied too long in the fiery depths. The darker blue patterns of the cheeks and brow may refer to the Fire God, Xiuhtecuhtli, whose name also means Turquoise Lord – he is sometimes shown adorned with turquoise mosaic and a nose ornament in the form of an identifying butterfly emblem.

**Limestone bust of the Young Maize God.
Maya, Copán, Mexico, AD 680–750.
Ht 90 cm, w. 54 cm.**

The Popol Vuh, the sacred book of the Maya, recounts a creation story that tells how the world came into being and how the gods created the first humans out of maize – a staple crop among the Maya. The Young Maize God is depicted here upon his emergence from the Underworld as the embodiment of vigorous fresh growth, marking the beginning of the annual agricultural cycle of renewal. (See also pp. 86–7.)

Many similar busts were used as architectural embellishments on Temple 22 at Copán. Rather than being fashioned from a single block of limestone, the heads were sculpted separately from the torsos, and close inspection of this well-known version reveals differences in colour, graining and surface texture. The head is also disproportionately large compared with the narrow shoulders and slender torso. This disparity may have been intentional or might indicate that this particular head and torso were not originally meant to fit together but were 'restored' in the late 19th century.

Gold diadem with embossed face.
Siguas culture, Peru, 1st–3rd century AD.
Ht 23.5 cm.

The central image on this object is a disembodied head with large round eyes and outstretched arms. Beneath the mouth, a pattern of parallel vertical embellishments may represent a beard, and a continuous row of embossed circles – possibly droplets of water – runs round the outer edge. Other similar figures have tear-lines visible on their cheeks and could be very early manifestations of the figure still described today in popular lore as the Andean Thunder God Tunupa – a celestial deity who controls the weather. The perforations visible around the head suggest that the object was sewn on to a textile backing and worn as a diadem affixed to a turban or headdress. They may have been used by rulers to proclaim their supernatural powers and may also have adorned the mummy bundles of deified ancestors.

Textile with seated figure.
Painted cotton. Muisca, Colombia (Gachansipa), 14th–15th century AD.
W. 137 cm.

Striking painted textiles were once traded throughout Muisca territory in the Andean cordilleras of central Colombia. Organic materials decompose rapidly in the humid conditions found there and this rare example may have been preserved as part of a suite of funerary objects interred in a dry cave or shaft and chamber tomb. It offers an unusually detailed glimpse of the structure and content of indigenous cosmology. The alternating panels of geometric patterns feature diagonal, interlaced strands that may be inspired by the kind of woven mat used for sitting on special occasions. Embedded within these are interlocking designs and spiral motifs that are matched on Muisca pottery and stone objects. The seated frontal figure adopts a 'displayed' pose with outstretched limbs and has a pronounced rayed halo-like design surrounding its head, perhaps indicating solar attributes. The orientation of the seated figure varies systematically across the textile. Extrapolating from this incomplete fragment, it would seem to have been repeated thirteen times in total.

Zoomorphic ceramic vessel.
Huaxtec, Mexico, 10th–15th century AD.
Ht 21.5 cm, diam. 22 cm.

At first glance, with its splayed legs and upturned head, the creature portrayed on this vessel might be identified as a turtle. As amphibians, turtles move freely between water and land and are frequently observed on beaches and mud banks at the interface between the two. The turtle's hard, domed carapace surfacing in lagoons and river settings provided an appropriate visual metaphor among the lowland Maya and Gulf Coast cultures for creation stories that describe the emergence of the earth from a primordial sea. However, the snout, pronounced round eyes, and long tail are typical of the opossum – a marsupial that carries its young in a pouch and is associated with birth and credited with medicinal properties in Mesoamerican lore. A water possum is later used as a name glyph for the Aztec ruler Ahuitzotl (see p. 97).

Bird standing atop a turtle.
Wood. Taíno, Greater Antilles,
15th–16th century AD. **Ht 65.5 cm.**

Taíno oral traditions from the Caribbean tell how humans came to be divided into men and women. This object shows a long-beaked wader – probably a grey heron – standing on top of a turtle. The bird has human toes that identify him as a 'bird-man' and potential husband for the 'turtle-woman' wife. The turtle's neck and head are inclined vertically upwards to touch and perhaps be fed by the bird's beak. Originally the eyes and beak would probably have been emphasized by the kind of shell inlay still visible on other Taíno sculptures (see p. 26).

The circular canopy or tray (most of which is now lost) at the top of the vertical support rising from the bird's back was used to hold a powdered snuff known as *cohoba*, made by grinding up the hallucinogenic seeds of a shrub (*Anadenanthera peregrina*). After careful ritual preparations including fasting and abstinence from sex, priests would inhale the powder nasally to produce powerful hallucinogenic visions revealing knowledge of the spirit world (see pp. 108–9, 118–19).

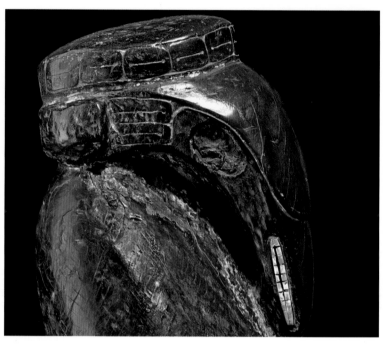

Bird-man spirit.

Wood. Taíno, Jamaica, 15th–16th century AD. Ht 87 cm.

This tall powerful sculpture combines both human and zoomorphic elements. The prominent beak and extended wings identify him as a bird, probably alluding to the idea of shamanic flight. However, the sexual organs of birds are not normally visible and the exposed genitals of this figure indicate that he is masculine. The detail of the head shows that inlaid shell once marked the eyes and still survives in the beak representing teeth, another human characteristic. He wears a headband embellished with a row of decorative elements that may represent shell plaques. This spirit being (*cemi*) of a bird-man seems to embody the archetypal husband whose long beak is celebrated in myths and folktales as the instrument for activating the reproductive potential of 'proto-women', creating sexual beings to ensure the continuity of the social group.

Male spirit being.
Wood. Taíno, Jamaica, 15th–16th century AD.
Ht 104 cm.

This imposing Taíno sculpture stands in a rigid frontal pose of hallucinogenic possession, signalled by the grimacing teeth and tears streaming down his cheeks. The ostentatious display of the sexual organs, emphasized by the hands resting on the hips, underlines its aggressive masculinity. The bulging calves are an admired manifestation of strength and durability produced by wearing ligatures bound beneath the knees and around the ankles.

Like most of the other surviving wooden objects, it is carved from the dense, black, tropical hardwood, guayacan (*Guaiacum officinale* L.). The prepared surface was polished with rounded river pebbles to bring the wood resin to the surface and help achieve an alluring deep black lustre.

On the back (not visible), the exposed skeletal vertebrae of the spinal column reinforce its association with the spirit world of revered dead male ancestors imbued with a life force called *cemí* that could assume different forms, invisible as well as visible. In this animate universe the Taíno actively sought contact with these potent and influential beings who were capable of performing formidable deeds. Many had names, titles, even genealogies, and with each interaction between object and person the *cemíes* added to their biography (see pp. 28, 108–9, 119).

Male spirit being.
Wood. Taíno, Jamaica, 15th–16th century AD.
Ht 39.5 cm.

This is a smaller version of the standing figure (*cemi*) described on p. 27. It also once had shell inlay in the eyes and mouth and the facial features are rendered with remarkable sensitivity. Both figures are carved in the same style, sharing an aggressive sexual pose with splayed legs and enlarged calves. The resemblance is close enough to suggest that they may even have been shaped by the same sculptor. Similar kinds of male sculptures might have been made to reflect aspects of male kinship and lineage relations. The exaggerated size of the male organ seems intended to call upon the virile, generative powers of the ancestors whose sexual potency underpinned the very existence of the community and was needed to assure its future well-being and vitality. They were evidently protagonists in the *cohoba* ceremony. This figure grasps a cylindrical object in either hand that may be *maracas* (rattles) which accompanied the rhythmic chants and exhortations common to shamanic rites.

Opposite: **Ceramic female figurine.**
Panuco River, Mexico, 15th–10th century BC.
Ht 8.4 cm.

Small figurines are among the earliest expressions of figurative 'art' and appear independently in Formative traditions elsewhere in the Americas (see p. 40). Exquisitely crafted

female figures show pronounced hips and breasts with careful attention to the detailing of the hair, ear spools and necklaces. They invite comparison with the so-called Venus fertility figures of the European Palaeolithic. This woman holds her hands clasped to a swelling belly and even at this scale her contemplative facial expression conveys the sense that she is reflecting upon the new life gestating within. Groups of miniature female figurines found in Formative burials may have been used in household shrines and fertility rituals.

Ceramic bowl in the form of a reposing woman.
Casas Grandes culture, Paquimé, Mexico, AD 1280–1450. Ht 12.6 cm.

The great trading centre of Casas Grandes in the desert reaches of northern Mexico was a key point of contact between the Pueblo cultures of what is today the southwestern United States and Mexican civilization to the south. The lively interaction between these two spheres of influence helped spawn a distinctive aesthetic tradition that finds expression in a combination of sensuous modelled forms with bold geometric, polychrome designs.

The accomplished execution and intriguing subject of this vessel beg close attention. The supine pose and closed eyes suggest that she has fallen asleep with legs drawn up, head nestling in a crooked left arm, and with her right arm resting across her chest. She wears a black armband and red wristbands, and the chevron painted on her cheeks may be an identifying clan emblem.

Her carefully groomed and tightly tonsured hair seems to be held in place at the back by a segmented headband. The rectangular design on her front probably represents the woven pattern displayed on her skirt. It is based on the principle of rotational symmetry, contraposing identical motifs around a central, diagonal axis composed of two parallel rows of zigzags. The overall effect suggests the channelling and controlling of charged energies to productive ends.

3

Becoming Human

The cultures of the Americas found diverse ways of recognizing and celebrating significant stages in the human life cycle. The range of small figurines of women with children reflects women's primary responsibility for suckling and nurturing the newborn. Very young children were considered 'wild', undisciplined and in need of training before they were ready to assume social responsibilities in a civilized society. Some Olmec figurines have a head with jaguar-like attributes superimposed on a seated baby's body, alluding to this undomesticated 'pre-human' condition.

Entry into the human world was marked in different ways. These included haircutting and naming, usually at around two years old when

Miniature seated figure.
Ivory, Eskimo-Aleut, Alaska, USA, c. AD 1779.
Ht 2.5 cm.
This tiny figure carved from walrus ivory was originally fitted to a bent wood hunting visor or helmet. Men carved ivory during the long Arctic winter nights – a time for conversation, contemplative reflection and retelling stories of clan origins, culture heroes, hunting adventures and feats of bravery. (See p. 41.)

a child was learning to walk. From then on the early years were spent close to the village supervised by women. There is good evidence to suggest that pre-pubescent young children were considered 'without sin' and not fully conscious or responsible for their own actions. At the onset of puberty in many societies children of around the same age were classified together as an age class – a group of peers who henceforth would face induction into the world of adult responsibilities together. We know more details of these rites from societies which still maintain their traditional practices than we can learn through archaeology, although certain objects offer suggestive glimpses of ritual events that were usually hidden from public view. Initiation into this new young adult world was an arduous and exacting process marked by solemn rites of passage that taught the participants, both boys and girls, esoteric lore about the mysteries as well as the practicalities of life. For instance, noviciates were obliged to confront intimidating masked figures impersonating spirit beings and to prove their fortitude and endurance by overcoming often painful ordeals. Among some Amazonian groups young boys must bear the excruciating stings of ants without a murmur of complaint and then, tutored by elder males, master the tracking skills that would ensure success in the hunt. With the onset of their menstrual cycle girls were taught their complementary roles by senior female relatives. Initiation rituals were soon followed by the search for suitable marriage partners, who had to demonstrate their fitness to assume family responsibilities. Early Spanish chroniclers record how young male Inca initiates took part in competitive races to a mountain top overlooking the Valley of Cusco and had their ears pierced to receive ear spools as a sign of their sexual maturity. Initially these ornaments were made of wood but were replaced with ever more precious materials as their wearers rose in seniority and rank (see ch. 6).

Connections to the land helped forge an enduring sense of belonging while networks of family, extended kin and lineage also bound communities together. Visual emblems in the form of badges and crests helped identify close family and clan, and shared language, customs and dress helped to define and declare allegiance in the face of competition from rivals for territory and resources (see ch. 4). Community survival, especially in harsh environments, often depended on co-operation and teamwork. The largest building in many communities, whether Algonquian 'long house' or Amazonian *maloca*, was built through collaborative endeavour and was the focus of local life and the setting for communal events. In many societies, collective identity was expressed by participation in drinking and smoking rituals that reinforced group membership and solidarity. These activities could also be used to negotiate relations and forge alliances with other clans and neighbouring groups.

Scene of a woman giving birth, Teozacoalco Annals (Zouche-Nuttall screenfold). Painted deerskin, Mixtec, Mexico, 15th–16th century AD. Ht 19 cm, w. 23.5 cm (each page).

The Teozacoalco Annals are one of a group of vividly informative screenfolds from towns in the Mixteca region of western Oaxaca. They record the genealogies of rival families over many generations and illustrate the deeds of specific rulers identified by name glyphs, including Eight Deer Jaguar Claw who ruled in the 11th century (see pp. 66–7). Place-signs and day-signs provide the location and date for many of the main episodes in the narrative such as births, succession to office, marriages, war, conquests and deaths.

The scene illustrated in detail here shows Lady Five Flint, whose serpent insignia floats behind her, giving birth to an heir, still attached by the umbilical cord. This event takes place on the day Three Flint of the year Three Flint, indicated by the glyphs beneath and at top left of the blue roundel. She then disappears head first into an opening – presumably a cave – in the side of a mountain, identified by diagonal bands, with four priests in attendance.

Ceramic figurine of a woman in festive attire with a child.
Classic Veracruz, Mexico, 4th–12th century AD.
Ht 15.7 cm, w. 10.5 cm.

This woman is depicted with legs akimbo and outstretched arms. On her right shoulder appear the head, one arm and feet of a young child she is carrying on her back, probably wrapped in a shawl under her mantle. The woman's pose and rich attire, including an oval necklace pendant and elaborate feather headdress, suggest she may be a participant in a public event such as a festival. Her headdress and eyes have been daubed with black *chapopote*, a blend of tar and rubber often applied to figurines dedicated to the earth deity. Her *quechquemitl* (woven mantle) and skirt are decorated with different motifs (see p. 113). The mantle is adorned with a pair of birds with outstretched wings, perhaps referring to migrations marking critical moments in the seasonal cycle. The figurine also functions as a whistle (see pp. 80–1).

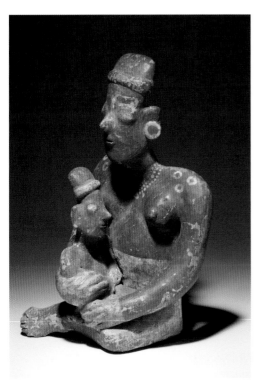

Ceramic figurine of a seated woman holding a child.

Nayarít, West Mexico, 3rd century BC–3rd century AD. Ht 21 cm, w. 12.5 cm.

A young child sits in the nurturing embrace of its mother's lap. They wear similar headbands and have the same elongated head. This reflects the practice of applying a tight binding around the cranium from a very early age, gradually modifying it so as to achieve the desired shape. The mother wears a wraparound skirt and prominent circular ear spools, and symbols are painted on her neck and shoulders to represent a necklace and other body ornamentation (see p. 38).

**Ceramic figurine of a seated woman holding a dog.
Nayarít, Mexico, 3rd century BC–3rd century AD.
Ht 54 cm, w. 26 cm.**

Though otherwise naked, this young woman is depicted with her hair carefully combed and parted and wearing a large nose ring as well as earrings, necklace and armbands. She is seated on a stool rather than directly on the ground, a sign of her status and prestige within the community (see p. 83). The scarification pattern on her shoulders and upper arms was a popular form of body ornament. With her left hand she holds a plate that rests on her shoulder, and a small dog nestles in the crook of her right arm. She leans forward with her mouth open as if intently absorbed in chanting or singing. Collective song and dance was a powerful means of asserting shared traditions and beliefs.

**Limestone figure of an old man and boy.
Huaxtec, Mexico, 10th–15th century AD.
Ht 34 cm.**

The wrinkled features and stooping posture of
this old man suggest that he represents a
community elder – perhaps a personification of
the aged Huaxtec thunder god Mam. His hands
are clasped protectively around the shoulders
of a naked young boy who stands tensely
clutching his abdomen. They may be engaged
in the kind of formal presentation ceremony
common to many cultures as part of 'coming of
age' rituals involving the induction and initiation
of pubescent boys and girls into their peer
group. The elder wears elongated pendant
earrings, a neatly arranged loincloth and cape,
and he appears to be grinning broadly. Other
versions of this old man show him holding a
serpent staff or dibble stick, used to penetrate
the earth so that it can receive new seed. Similar
sculptures are still used today as the focus of
ceremonial life in remote rural villages in Mexico.
At planting time they are bedecked with
greenery and flowers and people entreat them to
ensure the fertility of their fields and a bountiful
harvest.

Seated figurine.

Kaolin clay pottery, Olmec, Mexico,

12th–5th century BC. Ht 15.5 cm.

Mexico's Gulf Coast lowlands were the setting for the rise of the first widespread style in Mesoamerica in objects ranging from monumental stone sculpture to smaller, portable pieces in different media (see p. 136). The use of fine white kaolin clay gives this figurine a life-like quality and traces of a vivid red pigment that was applied on top of the white slip are also still visible. One rare find of a group of Olmec figurines, excavated in situ, revealed standing figures arranged in a semicircle, apparently engaged in an act of collective veneration or worship. This figure may once have formed part of such a scene.

Seated figure.

Soapstone (steatite), Northwest Coast, Strait of Georgia tradition, USA, 1st–9th century AD. Ht approx. 20 cm.

As in many other figurine traditions in the Americas, this piece seems intended to replicate in miniature some aspect of social and spiritual life that was especially significant for the community (see pp. 29, 32, 128–9). It is carved in soft soapstone with additional incised detailing of the head and hands. The encircling arms form a receptacle and the object may represent, or perhaps have been used in, shamanic or puberty rites.

Wampum gorget.

Algonquin, Ottawa, Canada, AD 1700–1820.

L. 114 cm, w. 17 cm.

Prestigious items were worn as symbols of male status. Many were crafted from wampum, made of strung beads woven into combinations of figurative designs and abstract motifs and invested with meaning that was shared by makers and owners. This composite ornament was designed to be worn with the circular shell gorget on the chest and the two panels of quillwork hanging down the back. The gorget was fashioned from a large species of marine shell – probably conch – and likely to have been traded in from the warm waters of the Gulf of Mexico. Attached to it are skin thongs with imitation-wampum straps, woven with a dark blue background punctuated by white flashes. The design on the back panels consists of a pair of black thunderbirds (see also p. 61) with outstretched wings outlined in white on an

orange background. Above, a jagged bolt of white and blue lightning zigzags energetically over the heads of the two birds from the wing-tip of one to the wing-tip of the other. The panel is edged in red stroud cloth (wool), followed by an alternating band of black and white imitation-wampum beads. Below the panel are two series of quill-wrapped thongs ending in metal (possibly zinc) cones filled with orange hair.

Painted horse-hide.
Patagonia, Aonikenk (Tehuelche), 19th century AD.
L. 179 cm, w. 185 cm.

As in other nomadic hunting cultures of the Americas, the preparation and painting of hide cloaks is a millennia-long tradition on the vast expanses of the Patagonian steppe grasslands. The painted designs have their roots far back in prehistoric times, for similar motifs are found both in rock art and on portable objects. The dense, continuous pattern of interlocking abstract motifs has been interpreted as a symbolic expression of kinship ties and group solidarity among the Aonikenk and their forebears. Originally the cloaks were made by sewing together as many as a dozen skins of young guanaco (*Lama guanicoe*), prized for their suppleness and warmth. With the introduction of the horse by European colonists, single hides painted with red, yellow and blue mineral pigments began to be produced, perhaps in response to trading opportunities rather than as a practical item of apparel for the makers.

**Wooden ceremonial steering board.
Ica, South Coast Peru, 12th–14th century AD.
Ht 168 cm, w. 23 cm.**

Unusual large, heavy objects like this are thought to have served as steering devices on ancient balsa sailing rafts. The rafts themselves were constructed by lashing together large balsa logs and erecting a mast and sail. Initial eyewitness accounts by Europeans suggest that a number of boards could be deployed by inserting and withdrawing them vertically to aid navigation. This example is made from the dense native hardwood huarango (*prosopis*).

Mastery of this maritime technology and hence control of an important means of long-distance trade and exchange must have conferred considerable prestige on coastal fishing communities. The orderly rows of sculpted figures, reinforced by the repetitive geometric designs beneath, convey a sense of the teamwork and interdependence that bound the crews together. These objects may also have been reused for other purposes such as grave markers.

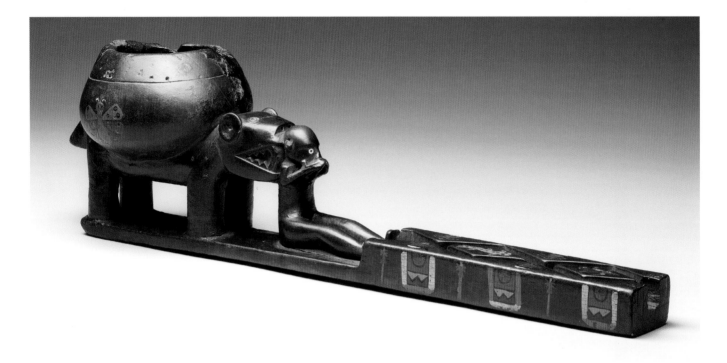

Wooden ceremonial drinking vessel (*paccha*). Inca-Colonial, Peru, late 17th–18th century AD. L. 48 cm, ht 14.5 cm.

This *paccha* is cleverly designed to circulate life-giving liquid. The bowl at one end on the puma's back is used to hold fermented maize beer (*chicha*). When tilted upward, the beer passes through a hidden, interior opening into the seated man, whose head is held by the puma's jaws. It then issues from between his legs to run down the zigzag channels on the handle. The painted figures of butterflies and frogs allude to Paititi, a mythical land of eternal abundance. Collective drinking rituals and inebriation provide a glimpse of this invisible paradise just beyond the harsh realities of everyday life (see pp. 88–9).

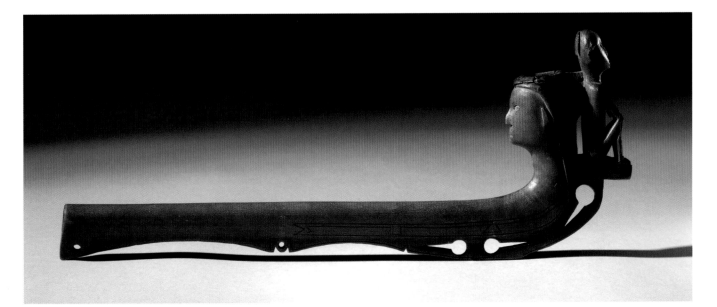

Wooden pipe.

Iroquois, New York, USA, AD 1700–1725.

L. 37 cm.

Just as the *paccha* opposite promotes the circulation of essential life energies in liquid form, so too this pipe channels spirit energies made visible in the curling wreaths of tobacco smoke. Like drinking, smoking was a collective ritual designed to cement alliances, and pipes themselves were sometimes gifted as a mark of respect. They are often carved with powerful images of ancestral clan leaders and probably became revered heirlooms. In this instance the smoker would face the embodied image of his ancestor and inhale smoke through the body of the figure. During communal smoking ceremonies the seated figure at the end of the pipe would face inward towards the circle of similarly seated participants.

Drinking chocolate at a wedding, Teozacoalco Annals (Zouche-Nuttall screenfold). Painted deerskin, Mixtec, Mexico, 15th–16th century AD. Ht 19 cm, w. 23.5 cm (each page).

This intimate scene shows an elaborately attired nobleman and woman with identifying name glyphs seated on jaguar pelts engaged in a formal ritual of exchange. On the left Lady Thirteen Skull proffers a vessel filled with foaming chocolate to Lord Thirteen Eagle of Teozacoalco. Made from cacao beans, chocolate was a prized commodity and may be a wedding dowry. The date glyph above Lord Thirteen Eagle's headdress places the event in the year Five Reed (AD 1039).

4
Roles and Responsibilities

Gender was often fundamental to assigning roles and responsibilities in many native societies throughout the Americas, though not always in ways familiar to us. Certain activities such as child-rearing were primarily reserved for females. Among lowland tropical societies women supervised many aspects of garden cultivation and the planting, harvesting and processing of staple crops such as manioc (cassava). In addition to the preparation and cooking of food, women were also responsible for brewing and serving large quantities of manioc beer at regular inter-communal gatherings. These events

Jadeite Eagle warrior.
Aztec, Mexico, AD 1300–1521. Ht 14.5 cm.
In Aztec mythology the eagle represented the power of the day and was believed to carry the sun into the sky from the underworld each morning. Eagle and Jaguar warriors, the two most prestigious military orders, were schooled in the art of war in special precincts in the heart of the Aztec capital Tenochtitlan. They earned status by performing feats of bravery and daring, notably securing captives for sacrifice. Warriors were awarded insignia such as cloaks, helmets and shields according to rank (see pp. 59, 130–31).

provided opportunities for negotiating social arrangements as well as feasting, fighting and exchanging goods. Important aspects of pottery making and weaving might be assigned specifically either to men or to women. In the South American highlands there is a long history of using llama and alpaca wool from domesticated herds, often managed by both men and women, which is paralleled by the cultivation of cotton on the coast and the use of reeds and other materials for woven basketry. The mining and smelting of metals also demanded hard-won knowledge and consummate skill. There is still much to learn about the chain of production and who was responsible for trade and exchange.

The most readily recognizable role in figurine imagery is the warrior, whether defensive or aggressive, bearing a club, lance or shield. A pervasive theme is the taking and conspicuous display of human 'trophies' such as the severed heads of enemies. There was competition for subsistence resources among mobile hunting groups and settled urban societies alike. The capture and despatch of defeated rivals assured supremacy and prestige and, with the absorption of the subject female population, fuelled the procreative potential of the victors. Among Plains Indians of North America, membership of warrior societies was secured by bravery in battle. Aztec men too had to prove their valour by defeating an enemy in personal combat before achieving the status of full adulthood. Both the Maya living in city states and later the Aztecs perfected the practice of waging war to secure captives for sacrifice on a large scale. Wooden spear-throwers (*atlatl*s) were used by hunting societies throughout the Americas from the Arctic to the Amazon. That an *atlatl* gilded with gold leaf was an essential item of ceremonial regalia for Aztec rulers testifies to its power as a potent symbol of the role of the ruler as a warrior-king.

Shamans and healers are heirs to a deep knowledge of the medicinal properties of plants and a long tradition of lore that can be traced back thousands of years. They are charged with the essential, perilous task of dealing with hidden forces of the spirit realm including potentially malevolent beings. Their ambiguous position is reflected in an ambivalent sexuality – shamans have been known to cross-dress, and the priests represented on Moche vessels had the same status as women in the social hierarchy.

As populations increased and fully fledged states evolved, a host of bureaucrats, administrators, scribes, priests and other functionaries attended the royal courts. Long-distance trading networks crossed land, river and sea, procuring an array of exotic raw materials from far afield to feed the growing demand for luxury goods. In Mesoamerica the Maya recorded the birth, accession and death of rulers in carved inscriptions that accompanied their images on stone stelae. Specially prepared deerskin and bark paper were also used to record and represent oral traditions. The Incas developed the *khipu* – a unique system of knotted cords that combined tactile qualities with colour coding – to co-ordinate the information about population and resources needed to administer their rapidly expanding empire. In towns and cities architectural space became more segregated in order to accommodate the royal lineage within palace settings and specialist craftsmen and women in production workshops as well as a priestly class devoted to maintaining calendrical knowledge and astronomical lore.

Ceramic vessel of a priest.

Moche, Peru, 2nd–8th century AD. Ht 46 cm.

Different offices are represented in the Moche social hierarchy, ranging from priests and warriors up to ruling lords. Items of costume and ornament provide intriguing clues to their identity, roles and responsibilities. This figure wears a chest ornament with a four-part stepped geometric pattern.

His headband is surmounted by a pair of attached monkeys with a chin strap to help keep the assemblage in place. Similar figures wear headbands adorned with birds or felines. A few actual examples have been excavated, which show that these depictions are realistic and accurate portrayals. Monkeys tend to be associated with the 'underworld' – a licentious and unruly realm that exists outside established cultural order with its codes of acceptable behaviour. Beneath a line traced across the chin hangs a row of flies emerging from their pupal cases, perhaps alluding to beliefs about the flies that mysteriously emerge from within corpses that have been left exposed to the elements following sacrifice. These associations help make the case for identifying this figure as a priest charged with mediating between the worlds of the living and the dead.

**Ceramic portrait vessel of Moche lord
'Long Nose'.**
Moche, Peru, 2nd–8th century AD.
Ht 24 cm, w. 13.5 cm.

Moche portrait vessels often have distinctive facial traits (see p. 103). This one, nicknamed 'Long Nose', has an unusually long, pointed nose. He has a vertical white stripe painted from his forehead to his chin, a narrow face and lens-shaped eyes – perhaps intended to emphasize his unusual nose. He wears a headband decorated with diagonal serrated motifs, large square ear ornaments and a multi-stringed necklace with beads of precious stones and shell below which hangs a pectoral ornament. He grasps in his left hand a small bag with a chequerboard design, probably used to hold coca leaves, and in his right hand holds a spatula.

Ceramic seated female figurine.
Tiwanaku, Bolivia, 7th–9th century AD.
Ht 15.5 cm, w. 8cm.

Few surviving Tiwanaku effigy vessels represent
human subjects in a naturalistic style (see
p. 105). This sensitive portrayal depicts a seated
woman with her lips pursed as though she were
whistling. Her hair is arranged in three long,
tapering tresses and she wears a long tunic with
short sleeves. On the front, executed in a
fugitive resist technique, rows of circles are
faintly visible and may represent a textile pattern.
A variety of precious polished stones including
lapis lazuli and malachite were used to fashion
the multiple strands of modelled and incised
beads around her neck and wrists. Her perforated
chin probably once held a lip plug made of a
perishable material, of which no trace is left. In
her right hand she grasps what may have been
a wooden or ceramic drinking vessel,
subsequently damaged (see pp. 88–9).

The vessel was collected in the mid
nineteenth century and is said to have come
from an island in Lake Titicaca. Recent
discoveries of a hitherto unexpectedly
sophisticated new style of Tiwanaku polychrome
pottery made on Pariti Island at the southern
end of the lake indicate this source is likely.
Shrines with high-quality buried offerings have
also been found elsewhere in Lake Titicaca such
as the islands of the Sun and Moon, important
pilgrimage destinations for the people of
Tiwanaku as well as later for the Inca.

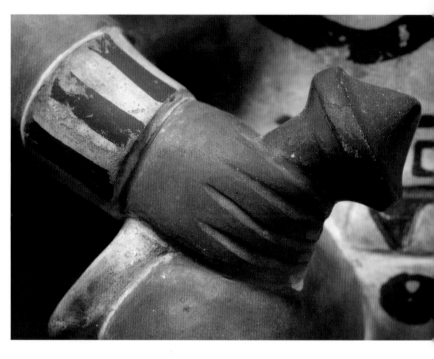

Ceramic warrior figurine.

Moche, Peru, 2nd–8th century AD. Ht 22.5 cm.

Warfare, warriors and prisoners are a recurring theme in Moche art and testify to violent inter-valley rivalries over valuable irrigable land. Warriors were the instrument of defence, domination and control – community identity and survival depended on a well equipped and suitably trained cadre of elite fighters. This figure with his alert gaze and fierce facial expression embodies all these qualities and belongs to a well-defined category of vessels which were mass-produced with only minor variations. He is wearing a white, sleeveless tunic, decorated with a dark red swirling pattern that also adorns his cone-shaped helmet, and a short loincloth with dark red dots, decorated belt and wrist-guards.

He is crouching on one knee with a circular shield on one arm and grips a club with a heavy stone mace-head in his right hand, ready for action or to serve as a sentry guarding palace entrances or staircases.

Excavations at Dos Cabezas yielded skeletons of so-called 'Moche Giants'. The wear on the bones and joints of these individuals is consistent with someone who maintained this specific pose for long periods over many years as a kneeling warrior. Other skeletal evidence reveals injuries sustained by blows from clubs as part of active war service. The vessels themselves seem to have served as symbolic tomb guardians, as they are found interred in large numbers in high-status burials (see pp. 62–3).

Ceremonial axe.

Wood and stone, Brazil, 19th century AD. Ht 79 cm.

Early historical collections have helped to preserve perishable materials in which Amazonian craftsmen once excelled, including a range of wooden clubs, spears, bows, canoes and paddles as well as fragile basketry and featherwork (see pp. 60, 122). This ceremonial axe is a rare example in which the combination of different media used in its manufacture have survived intact. The original fibre binding the stone axe-head to the long wooden handle is preserved, as are the motifs woven in basketwork. Sources of suitable stone are almost non-existent in the middle and lower Amazon, so the durable basalt from which this axe was fashioned would have been traded in from afar.

The end of the handle is surmounted by a powerful predatory bird, seen here in profile. The upstanding feather crest on its head and prominent circular bulge on its beak identify it as the harpy eagle (*harpia harpyja)*. This fearsome aerial predator descends without warning from the heights of the forest canopy to snatch prey such as the monkey, which here sits on its talons.

Ceremonial wooden *atlatl* (spear-thrower).
Aztec, Mexico, AD 1300–1521. L. 30 cm.

Among the arsenal of Aztec weapons were obsidian-bladed swords and an array of clubs, bows and arrows and spears. Perhaps the most prestigious was the spear-thrower known by its Nahuatl name *atlatl* and used to hurl lethal darts (see p. 77). This fine example still preserves traces of paper-thin hammered gold foil that was applied over both the front and back, and the beautifully worked supine body of a warrior carved along its length. It was probably intended for display and may have been part of a suite of ceremonial regalia proclaiming the role and status of the 'warrior king' (see p. 62). The warrior thrusts a spear with a pointed tip in front of him; just above the spear head, the head and two-forked tongue of a rattlesnake can be seen. The snake imagery refers to the ability of the owner to strike at a distance and was likened to the deadly lunge of the rattlesnake (see p. 7).

Wooden *macana* (war club).

Guiana, 19th century AD. L. 44 cm.

*Macana*s were fashioned from specially selected dense tropical hardwood that could deliver a death-dealing blow (see pp. 61, 63). The surfaces were highly polished then lightly incised with figurative images such as the hero twins shown in this example. These are complimented by abstract repetitive designs that share much in common with painted motifs found on pottery from northern Amazonia, including the Guiana lowlands.

The clubs were prestigious and treasured possessions used in dance and ritual as well as for fighting. As inter-group rivalries broke down under the effects of introduced epidemic diseases, the advent of metal weapons and firearms and the influence of European missionaries, clubs as the weapon of war slowly fell into disuse.

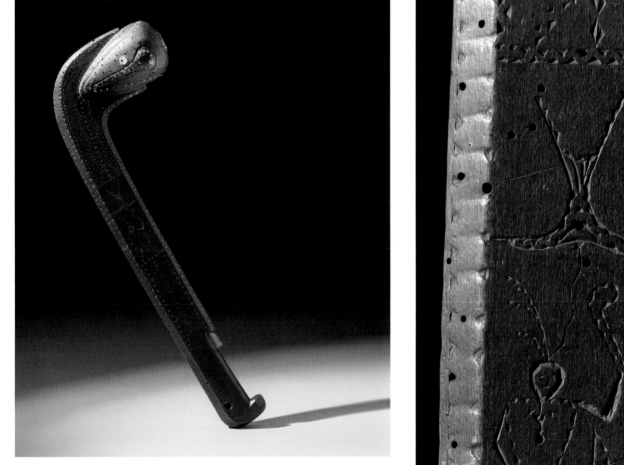

War club with thunderbird.
Wood and lead. Huron, Ontario, Canada, 18th century AD. L. 54 cm.
So-called 'ball-headed' clubs were the weapon of choice for combat at
close quarters. Inscribed into the surface by a process known as
'chip-carving' is the detail of a warrior holding aloft a similar club in one
hand and wielding a knife in the other. Above, a descending thunderbird
with outstretched wings emits a bolt of lightning that zigzags downwards
to strike the warrior's head beside his feathered headdress (see p. 42).
Glass beads and lead have been inlaid to add decorative details.

Gold pendant figurine.
Mixtec, Mexico, 12th–14th century AD.
Ht 8.5 cm.

Claims to hereditary nobility were based on tracing ancestral lineage and proclaiming military prowess through dress and ornament. Mixtec metalsmiths fashioned gold into prestigious objects that signalled their owners' status in life and at death accompanied them as tomb offerings. This image of a warrior-ruler was made by a process of low-wax casting, incorporating finely detailed false filigree work that defines the Mixtec gold style. Its small size makes the complexity of detail all the more remarkable.

The figure is richly adorned with an embellished headband, curved ear ornaments, a nose piece, and pendant plaques strung across his chest. On his left arm he bears a small circular shield, while with his right hand he grasps a serpent-headed sceptre or *atlatl* (spear-thrower, see pp. 59, 77). From a lip plug hangs a severed head – perhaps a war trophy – beneath which three pendant bells are suspended. The whole assemblage was apparently worn as a chest or lip ornament. The framing armature may represent a formal backdrop used on ceremonial occasions or simply serve to facilitate the fabrication and durability of the object.

Stone warrior with club and severed head. Costa Rica, 10th–15th century AD. Ht 54.5 cm, w. 32.5 cm.

Central America spawned a number of independent stone sculptural traditions taking advantage of a range of volcanic material that lent itself to shaping and detailing with harder stone hammers and chisels. On Costa Rica's Nicoya peninsula, both male and female subjects are represented in a narrow range of 'archetypal' poses – the women as an embodiment of feminine fertility and the men asserting their prowess as warriors. This figure wears a close-fitting head cap, ear spools and a patterned waistband but is otherwise naked. In his upraised right hand he brandishes an axe or club and with the other supports the severed head of a vanquished enemy – presumably the outcome of a successful raiding party. The sculpture is modest in size and seems to have been designed to be set in the ground, perhaps serving as a guardian figure at the entrance to a tomb.

Stone pipe fragment in the shape of a tattooed warrior head. Hopewell culture, Mound City, Ohio, USA, 2nd century BC– 1st century AD. Ht 4.3 cm.

Identifying tattoos are etched deeply into the facial features of this warrior. The one surviving elongated ear is pierced to receive an ear spool. The object was found among some two hundred pipe fragments in an offering cache deposited within one of the earthen platform mounds built by the Hopewell culture. Similar objects have been excavated from burial contexts, where they seem to have been deposited as trophies representing defeated rivals.

**Stone vessel with scenes of a contest
over a severed head.
Classic Veracruz, Mexico, 4th–12th century AD.
L. 55 cm, Ht 35 cm, w. 73 cm.**

The scenes carved on the four sides of this vessel depict two protagonists engaged in a formal contest over a severed head with a tasselled plume of long hair. The left-hand figure always wears a distinctive nose ornament that extends across his cheek, while the fanged jaws of his opponent emphasize his supernatural powers. Their confrontation is played out in a sequence of arm gestures which are the mirror image of each other, changing in synchronized fashion from scene to scene around the vessel, following the direction in which the severed head is facing. Subtle variations in the costume and headdress of each figure echo and elaborate upon the visual language of the arm gestures. It seems likely that the vessel held a liquid, perhaps *pulque*, the fermented beverage made from the juice of the *maguey* plant, which was consumed in large quantities at festivals (see p. 133). It probably served as a ritual object during a series of related ceremonies, among them the ball game, celebrated at designated times of the year.

Scenes showing Eight Deer's two water-borne attacks, Teozacoalco Annals (Zouche-Nuttall screenfold). Painted deerskin, Mixtec, Mexico, 15th–16th century AD. **Ht 19 cm, W. 23.5 cm (each page).**

These painted scenes form part of a historical narrative recounting the genealogy and deeds of Mixtec rulers and their families. The construction of significant monuments is also noted, as are occasional natural phenomena such as eclipses and disasters including floods, earthquakes and famines. One of the principal protagonists was the formidable Eight Deer Jaguar Claw who expanded his domain during the 11th century AD. At left Eight Deer, who hails from the town of Tilantongo, is pursuing an aggressive campaign against his rival Four Jaguar to settle a dispute. He has despatched warriors in canoes who are embarking on a night-time, water-borne attack. The assailants are traversing a calm stretch of water, signalled by the aquatic creatures below which are swimming in sympathy with the direction of the attack. A later daytime mission (above), also by canoe, ends in disaster due to bad weather and rough water, causing the boats to sink. However, this temporary setback does not deter Eight Deer from prosecuting further successful military ventures against his rivals and foes.

Weaving scene, fine-line painting on a pottery vessel. Moche, Peru, 2nd–8th century AD. Diam. 33.5 cm.

This fine-line painting of a weaving scene arranged around the inner circumference of a large flared bowl shows female weavers with back-strap looms surrounded by weaving implements such as spindles and spindle whorls. One end of each loom is suspended from the top of a vertical wall post. These posts support a thatched roof, suggesting that the artisans are gathered inside a special building housing a workshop or guild of weavers. Other elements in the background may be samples or finished products, and various forms of ceramic vessels are noted including the characteristic stirrup-spout vessel and flared drinking beakers. Males in elaborate dress are engaged in other (unspecified) activities, perhaps in courtyards outside. This is one of very few scenes illustrating the actual production of objects.

Opposite: **Red bag with double-headed bird motif. Dyed cotton and wool. Ica, Peru, 10th–15th century AD. Ht 34 cm, w. 26 cm.**

This bag is woven from a blend of cotton and camelid wool, the product of trade and exchange between the Peruvian south coast and the adjacent highlands. Cotton was one of the earliest domesticated crops and thrives in the coastal valleys. Altiplano herders managed huge numbers of llamas and alpacas, and as well as supplying meat and wool they were the main means of transport. Although it is a little larger than most used for this purpose, the bag may have served to hold coca leaves. Masticating a quid of coca leaves with lime powder helped mitigate the exhaustion and

stress brought on by sustained
physical effort, especially at high
altitude.

Decorative zigzag stitching runs
down the sides of the bag and
tassels of coloured camelid wool
yarn are attached at the bottom
corners. A repetitive pattern of
double-headed bird motifs runs
upwards and downwards in
alternating rows picked out in
a range of light and dark blue,
lilac and pink, with a bold
black outline. These are
framed by bands of
geometric motifs so that
the design covers the
whole available surface.

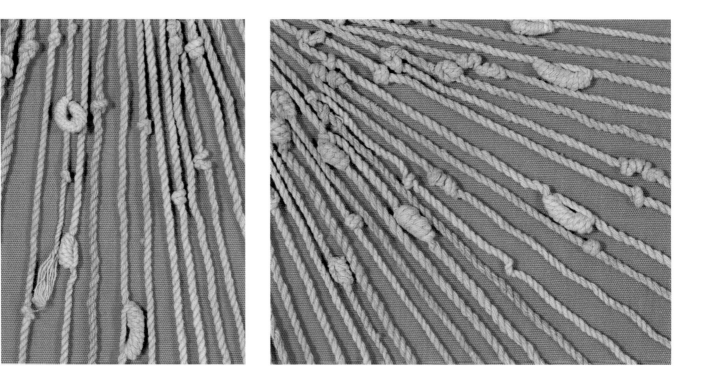

Cotton *khipu* (also *quipu*).

Inca, Peru, 15th–16th century AD. L. 74–104 cm.

The word *khipu* comes from the *Quechua* word for knot, and *khipus* are textile objects consisting of methodically arranged knotted and coloured cords woven in cotton and occasionally camelid fibre. They are composed of one primary cord with pendant cords and branching subsidiary cords attached. The numbers, positions and colours of the cords together with the numbers, direction and sequencing of different kinds of knots were all used to encode an immense amount of information. They were already known several hundred years earlier in Tiwanaku and Wari, but the Incas perfected their use as sophisticated accounting devices using a decimal system.

Khipus were portable, rolled up in a spiral to be stored and carried from one place to another. Specialized Inca administrators known as *khipucamayuq* were charged with responsibility for safeguarding these key instruments of imperial bureaucracy. They could read and interpret the stored data ranging from a population census to the taxation and tribute owed by towns and provinces. It is possible, though not yet proven, that they also record other kinds of information on genealogies, the agricultural calendar and perhaps even narrative traditions, all of which await decipherment. The knotting technique used on the *khipu* illustrated here indicates that it may be a 'narrative' type. After the Spanish conquest some few were translated into Spanish with the help of native informants and written down by a Spanish scribe. This process of *khipu* reading, translation and transcription was complicated by the differing interests of those involved. Some six hundred *khipus* of varying degrees of complexity have been preserved in museum collections and are currently the subject of intensive study.

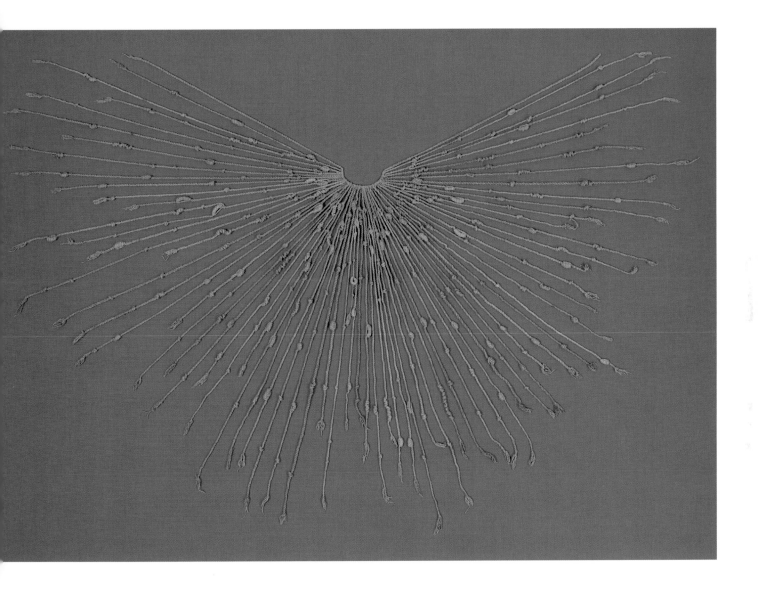

5

The Seasonal Cycle

The Americas north and south were the last continental land mass to be settled by modern humans. Conservative estimates infer that this only took place within the last 15,000 years, as the last Ice Age came to an end, while others suggest a much earlier arrival up to 50,000 years ago. Some Native American traditions assert that their ancestors emerged from the earth and have always inhabited recognized tribal territories. Certainly the first nomadic bands of hunters lived in a close, symbiotic relationship with the animals on which they depended. Regular seasonal encampments were set up along the routes of migratory birds and animals such as caribou in the sub-Arctic, buffalo on the Great Plains and guanaco in the steppe grasslands of Patagonia. Ingenious tools, weapons and hunting techniques were developed to exploit the possibilities afforded by particular ecological niches. Maritime, riverine, forest and grassland environments each offered an array of specialized food sources such as the annual run of migrating salmon on Canada's Northwest coast that provided a seasonal abundance of fish. This was complemented by conifer forests that supplied the raw material for an accomplished woodworking tradition embracing everything from canoes to dwellings that were marked by monumental sculptures rendering visible the animal ancestors of different clans. Dense stands of native oak in California's Sacramento Valley were harvested annually for acorns and in Amazonia a wide variety of trees and plants were exploited, ranging from peanuts to palm nuts.

The first settled village communities and the earliest evidence of pottery anywhere in the Americas are found on the bluffs and

Miniature gold llama.
Inca, Peru, 14th–15th century AD. Ht 6.3 cm.
Llamas are a vital source of meat and wool for altiplano communities as well as being pack animals. The size and health of its herds are a direct measure of a community's health and prosperity. Along with miniature human figurines (pp. 128–9), miniature gold llamas were deposited as offerings to accompany high-altitude human sacrifices to the mountain deities *apus* to ensure the arrival of the life-giving moisture that replenishes the altiplano grasses and promotes the fertility of the herds. (See p. 93.)

floodplain of the middle Amazon and at the mouths of the other great rivers of the lowland tropics. In the Andean *puna* (high grasslands), hunters co-existed with wild herds of camelids, eventually domesticating llamas and alpacas for meat, wool and a means of transport in this challenging environment. The domestication and spread of an array of new crops proceeded apace and productive new land was won by implementing sophisticated irrigation and terracing systems in both highland and coastal valleys. The growing dependence on potatoes and maize meant that the seasonal round of planting and harvest festivals galvanized the whole community, whose livelihood and well-being depended on these key staples.

The regeneration of plant life was driven by the alternating wet and dry seasons. Stunning Quimbaya gold figurines capture key moments in the rituals celebrated in the northern valleys of the Andean Cordillera in Colombia. These seasonal transitions signalled key turning points in the agricultural year and in many societies also determined the timing of the initiation rites that marked significant stages in the human life cycle (see ch. 3). The communal memory of hunting origins was often preserved in agricultural societies and ritual deer hunts are recorded in fine-line paintings on Moche vessels. Periodic fallow periods, when male labour was not otherwise engaged in essential agricultural pursuits, might also be the time for prosecuting rivalries, organizing raids and initiating warfare against other communities.

The transition from dry to wet season was especially important for desert dwellers and was a time of heightened ritual tension, when dances took place to entreat rain-bearing clouds to deliver their precious cargo. In highland Mexico the rain god Tlaloc was the principal agricultural deity and one of the twin shrines atop the Great Temple in the Aztec capital Tenochtitlan was dedicated to him. In the Andes a 'vertical archipelago' linked different altitudes, facilitating the exchange of highland products such as potatoes for maize from lower valleys. Although entirely different calendars were developed in Mesoamerica and the Andes, they shared the need to regulate the agricultural year in accordance with an enduring seasonal cycle.

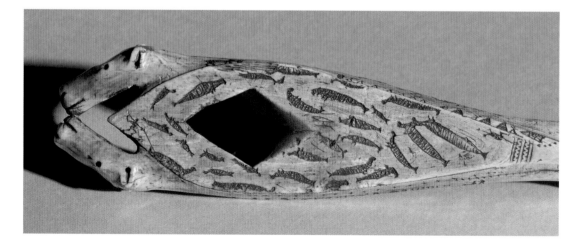

Walrus ivory arrow-straightener.
North Alaskan Eskimo, USA, *c.* AD 1850.
L. 18 cm, w. 5 cm.

Durable walrus ivory has been used to fashion this arrow-straightener in the form of foetal caribou. It is used by wedging the end of the arrow shaft inside the diamond-shaped cavity to gain leverage and apply pressure. Around the aperture walruses cavort in the water, one of which (at bottom left) is being harpooned. An array of other detailed hunting scenes is inscribed into the surface of every facet of the tool. In one, a herd of swimming caribou distinguished by their huge antlers is pursued by a hunter with upraised spear in a canoe towards a figure standing on the shore. Another scene shows a row of tents marking the site of a seasonal camp beside which a band of Eskimo with linked hands are engaged in a collective celebratory dance. A further encampment features game hanging from drying racks with a hunter at left loosing off an arrow at a skein of migrating geese flying overhead.

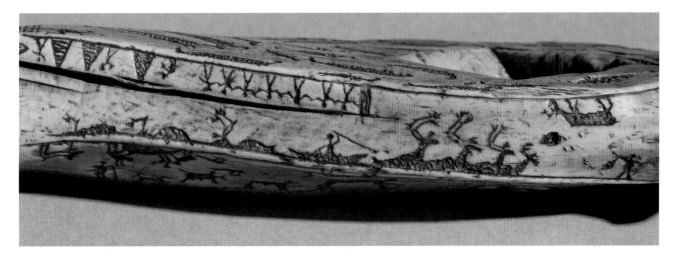

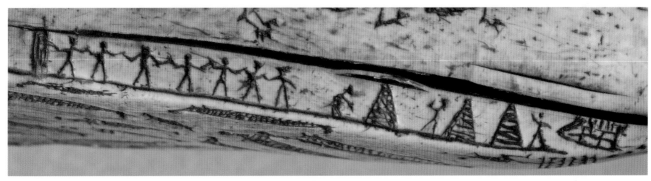

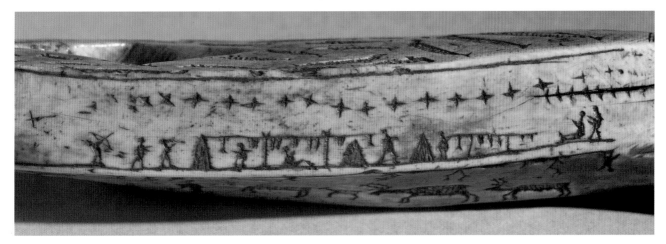

Reed basket with shell, glass and feather dangles.
Northern California, USA, *c*. AD 1770.
Ht approx. 10 cm.

The basketry of northern Californian cultures can be traced back thousands of years and in historic times the Chumash and Pomo gained renown for their technical mastery. Weaving skills were passed from generation to generation, gradually building a shared repertoire of patterns and designs that identify the traditions of each group and distinguish them from those of its neighbours and rivals. A combination of weaving technique and the use of dyes was used to achieve bold contrasts and characteristic geometric motifs such as the zigzag design running round the circumference of this piece. Additional external embellishments include pendant strings of glass beads and abalone shell interspersed with groups of small disks and red woodpecker feathers.

Wooden *atlatl* (spear-thrower).
Eskimo-Aleut, Nootka Sound, Canada,
18th–19th century AD. L. 47 cm.

Atlatls are devices used to enhance the power
and range achieved by hunters and warriors
when hurling spears and lances. One end of the
atlatl is held in the hand and the base of the
shaft is inserted in a cavity or groove at the
other end. By effectively extending the length of
the arm this improves the leverage and
increases the velocity of the projectile. *Atlatls*
have an ancient history and their antecedents lie
across the Bering Straits to Asia. Both land and
maritime hunting societies exploited their
considerable advantages and this helps explain
their widespread distribution and durability.

This Aleut example bears the engraved
image of a sea otter with upraised hands
clasped to its mouth, and three beads have also
been set into the upper surface. (See also p. 59.)

Modelled and painted ceramic vessel showing a deer hunt.
Moche, Peru, 2nd–8th century AD.
Ht 23 cm, w. 14.5 cm.

This vessel is surmounted by the figure of a young deer whose budding antlers suggest an early stage of growth. The pelt markings closely match those on the deer represented in the fine-line painted scene below, which features a ritual deer hunt in which the animal is being pursued on foot by a warrior attired in elaborate regalia, armed with a long-handled club and aided by a dog (not visible). Similar scenes on other vessels show nets being used to trap the animal as well as sand dunes and typical vegetation in what is clearly a desert setting. The emphasis is on close engagement with the quarry which, like defeated human captives, must shed blood in the course of being sacrificed. As an elite vessel from a tomb offering it likely represents a Moche lord proving his mettle as a hunter. The underlying meaning may lie in the analogy between the deer's shedding of its antlers and the cycle of seasonal agricultural renewal.

Ceramic vessel with two birds' heads.
Moche, Peru, 2nd–8th century AD.
Ht 22.5 cm, w. 26.5 cm.

Moche potters excelled at modelling realistic depictions of people, plants and animals. This vessel depicts a pair of long-necked birds with head crests, throat ruffs and diagnostic eye-markings. The inverted heads hang limply as if being carried home after a successful hunt. The graceful spout is typically Moche, but the execution of other incised decorative elements makes its attribution open to question. The studied symmetry of the piece would have had great appeal for a society in which concepts of duality were important.

Seated man playing flute.
Ceramic, Moche, Peru, 2nd–8th century AD.
Ht 25 cm.

This musician is meticulously attired with a neatly knotted headband, short-sleeved shirt and ear spools. The sleeve of his tunic is decorated with the distinctive 'step-wave' motif – a pervasive symbol in coastal Peruvian cultures that signified the juxtaposition of land and sea. The headband is decorated with a continuous row of kidney beans and has a serrated fringe.

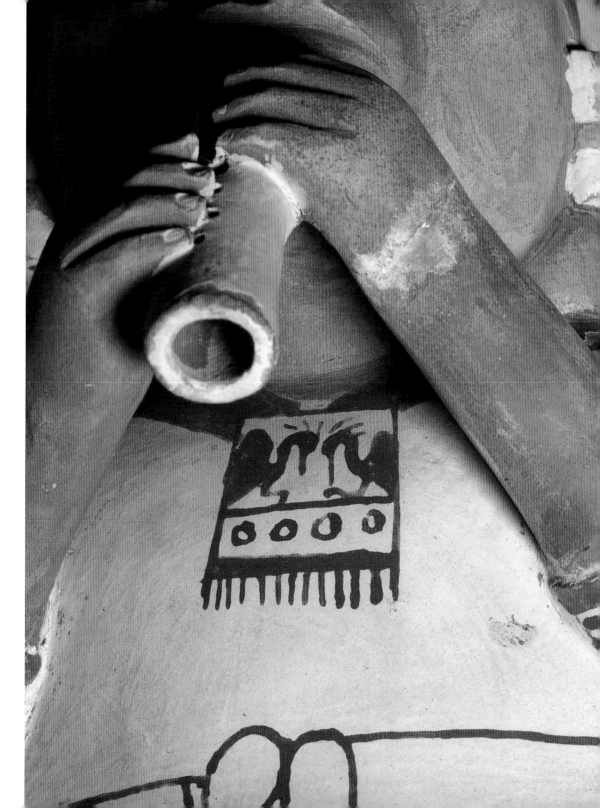

A pendant chest ornament bears a motif of a pair of birds. The man is playing a simple kind of duct-flute which has a high-pitched melodious warble and he may have been participating in a seasonal festival. The left hand has evidently broken off at the wrist and subsequently been restored in clay of a different colour.

**Gold alloy lime flasks (*poporo*).
Quimbaya culture, Colombia,
7th–11th century AD.**

Standing male figure. Ht 30 cm.

These objects count among the masterpieces
of pre-Columbian gold-working. Both were used
as containers for holding lime powder. The
protuberance on top of their heads has an
opening into which a spatula was inserted to
transfer the lime from the container and ingest it
little by little with a quid of coca leaves in the
mouth. This is sometimes represented as a
bulge in the cheek of modelled figurines
(see p. 128). The lime helps release the alkaloids
in the leaf that serve as an active stimulant and
to counteract the hunger pangs and exhaustion
brought on by sustained physical effort. The
flasks were made by a process known as
lost-wax casting with an alloy of gold and
copper core (*tumbaga*). An X-ray of the male
figure has revealed that the initial casting was
flawed – spaces where the metal did not flow
have left gaps in the solidified metal which were
subsequently filled by running in additional
molten metal.

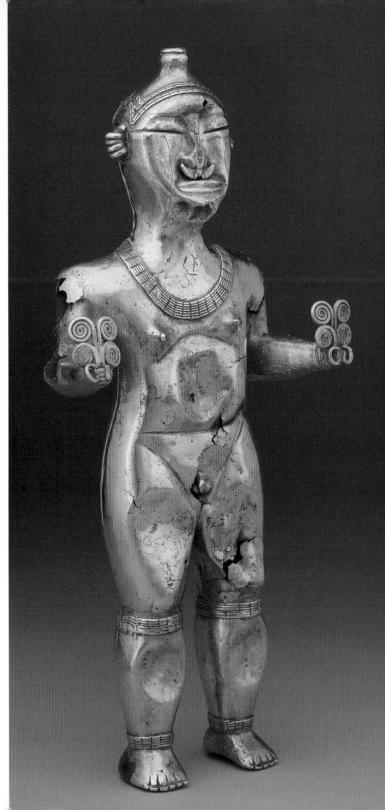

Seated female figure. Ht 14.5 cm.

The pose, facial details and body ornament of these figures have much in common and offer some clues to the nature of the ceremony itself. The male adopts a formal stance while, unusually for a woman, she is seated on a ritual stool indicative of her high status. Both figures are nude and wear ligatures just above the ankle and beneath their knees (see p. 27). Each wears a special kind of head cap with a decorated border, multiple earrings, a nose ornament and a stringed necklace. Their eyes are half closed as if to signal a contemplative state of mind and they hold spiral volutes in either hand. These might be interpreted as objects, but no actual examples like this are known. Conceivably they may allude to sprigs of sprouting vegetation which could have been carried or presented as part of seasonal fertility rites.

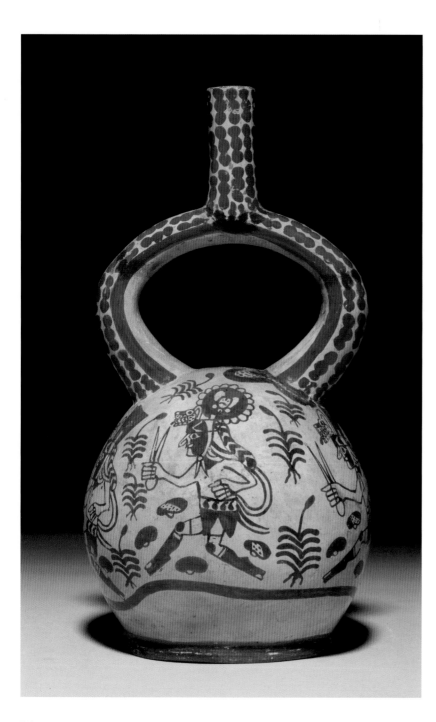

Ritual Runners, fine-line painting on a ceramic vessel. Moche, Peru, 2nd–8th century AD. Ht 27.5 cm, w. 15 cm.

Moche fine-line painted vessels feature selected themes that, with slight variations, appear repeatedly on many different pots. Well-known ones, named after the principal activity depicted, include the 'Burial Theme', in which a coffin is shown being placed in a deep shaft tomb, and the 'Presentation Theme', where goblets filled with the blood from a sacrificed captive are presented to a lord on a raised dais.

This vessel portrays a line of Ritual Runners processing around the circumference. The Runners wear a loincloth or short skirt and each carries a small cloth or bag with the ends pointing upwards. The detail at right shows a turban headdress with a fox head at the front and a large copper disc, secured by a neckerchief tied under the chin. At the back hangs a neck covering decorated with a pattern of nested chevrons, and from this a long ribbon loops down and is attached at the Runner's waist. The Runners traverse an undulating desert landscape indicated by heat-tolerant species such as the *Tilansia* shrubs represented on this vessel. A large bean identifiable as *Phaseolus vulgaris* is shown prominently in the scene. This was one among a suite of productive crops that flourished in the irrigated valleys and has led scholars to propose that the Runners are engaged in a Ritual Race bearing sprouting beans in their bags as part of seasonal fertility rituals (see p. 78).

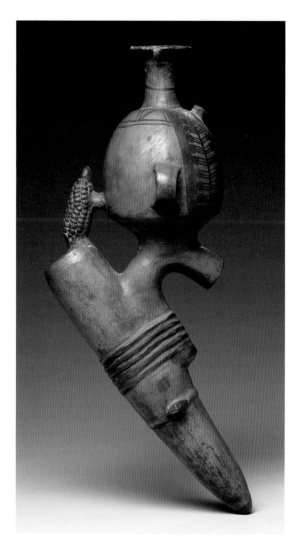

Ceramic ceremonial vessel (*paccha*) in the form of a digging stick (*chaquitaclla*).
Inca, Peru, 15th–16th century AD. Ht 42 cm.

The distinctive form of this rare kind of ceremonial object is based on the *chaquitaclla* – the traditional Andean foot plough – and offers intriguing clues to its meaning and function.

Each year the beginning of the agricultural cycle was announced by the ritual act of 'opening of the earth'. The Inca king as ruler of *Tahuantinsuyu* – 'the Empire of the Four Quarters' – was accompanied by the lords of the principal provinces. Wielding large foot ploughs, they broke the ground in unison accompanied by chanting, singing and drinking to mark *chacra yapuy quilla*, the festival of first planting.

The modelled representation of a growing maize cob on the *paccha*, together with the miniature *urpu* or storage vessel at the top, therefore encapsulates the whole agricultural cycle of maize from planting to harvest. Maize was originally domesticated in the highlands of Mexico and from there became an important staple food throughout much of Meso and South America. The *paccha* itself is hollow and has an opening at the top enabling *chicha* (fermented maize beer) to be poured in at one end and circulate through the vessel before escaping through a narrow orifice at the tip to symbolically irrigate and inseminate the earth. (See pp. 21, 97.)

Painted wooden beaker (kero) with feline and rainbow.

Inca-Colonial, late 17th–18th century AD.

Ht 18.5 cm.

In Andean culture powerful felines, especially the lowland jaguar, were associated with the entrances to the springs and subterranean waters of the paradise realm of Paititi. On this kero, a rainbow appears from the mouth of the feline as an extension of its whiskers. This relationship between the feline and the rainbow is part of ancient and modern Andean mythology linking felines and rain, seen here falling as white dots below the rainbow. Beneath the rainbow's arch stand the Inca (king) and Coya (queen; not visible), and in the lower register the nested squares represent the *ushnu*, a sacred space. It was and still is believed that jaguars are the doors of Paititi and that when the right moment comes, these doors will open, permitting access to Quechuas and no one else. While the *keros* are objects of the colonial period, the scenes featured on them express many persistent native beliefs about symbols of legitimate native authority and nobility in the face of the Spanish conquest.

Painted wooden beaker (*kero*) with dance scene.

Inca-Colonial, late 17th–18th century AD.
Ht 20.5 cm.

The dance of the Ch'unchus is a recurring theme on colonial *keros*. The Ch'unchus were held to be a ferocious tribe living in lowland Amazonia and the guardians of the legendary lands and cities such as Paititi or El Dorado. The theme is illustrated following a carefully prescribed layout: the dancers appear in single file, with a flag-bearer at the front of the group carrying a large banner patterned with multi-coloured squares. Behind the flag-bearer are two musicians playing the bugle and tambourine. There is always one black individual – by this time Africans had already been brought to the Americas. In procession behind the musicians are dancers with feather headdresses, large tunics or *unkus*, below which they wear trousers. Only the musicians wear Spanish attire. Flowers and small animals (parrots, macaws or small snakes) complete this lively scene of a seasonal harvest festival celebration. (See pp. 90–91.)

Cotton armorial tapestry.
Colonial Peru, late 18th century.
L. 244 cm, w. 216 cm.

The designs on this tapestry combine indigenous with colonial Spanish motifs. The coat of arms at the centre is obviously European, but it has not been linked to any known family of the Spanish conquistadors. A central panel is filled with mermaids or sirens playing a variety of musical instruments, surrounded by lush vegetation, birds and animals – a picture of vitality and fertility. Surrounding this is a border showing hunters with guns and wearing European-style attire. The outer border represents the Inca nobility.

Kings with staffs, headdresses and sun-shaped gold medallions are attended by women holding a pair of wooden drinking beakers (keros) (see pp. 88–9). An architectural feature is represented at the top and bottom of the tapestry, perhaps a church entrance as indicated by the arched windows and columns. The multi-coloured chequered flags flying on the building recall the banners seen on the wooden keros (p. 89). This combination of figures drinking from keros and playing musical instruments, and the banners, conveys the spirit of festivity and ceremony also portrayed on the wooden keros themselves.

Carved stone vessel (*cocha*).
Inca, Peru, 16th century AD.
Ht 18 cm, diam. 50 cm, w. 67 cm.

This massive stone vessel retains the traditional form of Inca ritual vessels of a similar large size that are usually carved with spiralling serpents (see p. 15). This piece is apparently unique as the only example so far known, which is inscribed with figurative scenes that were probably applied in the early colonial period. Likewise the rounded form of the handles differs from the pre-Columbian examples, and these shifts in style and content are similar to those found on *keros* of the pre-contact on into the early colonial period (see pp. 88–9).

On one side a large central solar disc with a face is flanked by two standing figures with their hands to their chest. Directly beneath the solar disc there are two opposed kneeling figures with their hands clasped in front of them and

a small diamond-shaped object with a schematic face standing between them. This small cult figure appears to be the earthly manifestation or representative of the solar deity. No actual objects like this were known until recent finds of conical stone objects in association with Inca *ushnu* platforms.

On the obverse side of the vessel a complementary scene has a male and female figure at centre – possibly the Inca and his *coya* – who are the focus for a procession comprising a woman with a spindle, a hunchback and llamas being led in from either side. Together the whole is likely to represent key times – perhaps planting and harvest festivals – in the Inca agricultural calendar.

Ceramic funerary vessel.
Zapotec, Mexico,
5th–7th century AD.
Ht 20.5 cm, w. 13.5 cm.
Funerary urns representing revered ancestors were buried with deceased rulers in tombs surrounding the central plaza of the Zapotec capital, Monte Albán. The seated figures wear masks and headdresses embodying supernatural forces and beings such as the storm or thunder god. Some are identified by year signs and name glyphs taken from the 260-day ritual calendar that are displayed on the chest ornament. The tombs were visited repeatedly over many generations as the focus for royal ancestor worship. Offerings of burning incense, fresh blood, chocolate and fermented *pulque* were made to entreat the ancestors to intercede favourably in human affairs.

Stone Xiuhcoatl (Fire Serpent).
Aztec, Mexico, AD 1400–1521.
Ht 77 cm, w. 60 cm.

The Aztecs conceived of heat and fire in many guises. This dynamic work captures the instant when Xiuhcoatl as a sky 'dragon', with clawed limbs and fanged jaws agape, strikes from on high. It embodies the potent discharge of energy that takes place when lightning as a jagged, serpentine bolt of fire plunges earthward from the heavens. The figure's tail is formed by the conventional symbol for the Mexican year (*xihuitl*) comprising a triangle and two entwined trapezes. It was probably originally incorporated into a temple façade, perhaps flanking a stairway.

Mask of Quetzalcoatl or Tlaloc.
Turquoise mosaic on wood. Mixtec-Aztec,
Mexico, 15th–16th century AD.
Ht 17.3 cm, w. 16.7 cm.

This mask is believed to represent Quetzalcoatl
(the 'feathered serpent' god of sky and creation)
or the rain god Tlaloc, both associated with
water and with serpents.

The relief design incorporates two serpents,
one worked in pale green turquoise and one in
blue, which encircle the eyes and are entwined
over the nose and around the mouth. Plumed
serpent tails hang at the temples on either side.

The Spanish friar Bernardino de Sahagún,
writing in the 16th century AD, describes a mask
like this one among the gifts given by the Aztec
emperor Moctezuma II to the Spanish captain
Hernán Cortés upon his first arrival on Mexican
shores.

Carved stone box with an image of Tlaloc.
Aztec, Mexico, AD 1400–1521. L. 19 cm, ht 23 cm, w. 34.5 cm.

Stone boxes called *tepetlacalli* (meaning 'stone house') were among the most treasured personal possessions of Mexica rulers. They were used as containers to guard ritual implements employed in self-sacrifice to draw blood, as well as to hold offerings and the ashes of deceased rulers. They were carved in relief on all sides.

The most complete scene shown here features the horizontal figure of Tlaloc, the Aztec rain god. He is wearing a shimmering feathered crown and in his outstretched arms holds an everted jar from which pours a stream of water with ears of maize and seashells to fertilize the earth. On the reverse of this scene is an *ahuitzotl*, a mythical aquatic animal similar to a water possum with a long coiled tail, which was used as a sign to represent Ahuitzotl, who ruled from AD 1486 to 1502. This box was therefore likely to have belonged to him.

6

Rulers and Rulership

Most of the named and identified images that have survived of rulers in the pre-Columbian Americas are in fact later representations, executed in a figurative Western style that developed after contact with Europeans. They feature specific emblems and insignia that proclaimed the exalted status of ruling lords and kings. The Inca king was entitled to wear a headband bearing three vertical plumes (*llauto*), though unfortunately no examples have survived. The Aztec *huey tlatoani* ('great speaker') wore a small triangular headpiece inlaid with precious turquoise and also had a stone box with his identifying glyph which held personal heirlooms and blood-letting instruments (see p. 97). On Maya stelae individual rulers are portrayed celebrating accession rituals and are named in the accompanying glyphic texts. A comparable Aztec example is the now largely destroyed full-length 'portrait' that Moctezuma II ordered to be carved in bedrock at the foot of Chapultepec Hill, not far from the capital Tenochtitlan. Original 'portraits' of rulers in a naturalistic style are extremely rare. Among pre-Columbian traditions, Moche portrait vessels bearing the signature 'stirrup spout'

have been thought to represent a realistic likeness of recognizable individuals whose titles and names will always elude us (see opposite).

A range of precious materials was incorporated into the elaborate costume and ceremonial regalia that signalled the powers and attributes of chiefs, lords and kings. Featherwork was deployed to spectacular effect within traditions ranging from the North American Plains to Amazonia and central Brazil. The unmistakable long, blue-green iridescent tail feathers of the Mesoamerican *quetzal* adorned the headdresses worn by Maya lords. This was paralleled in South America by the vibrant plumage of other sought-after tropical birds such as the toucan, macaw and various species of hummingbird, with their intense hues of red, yellow and blue. These were complemented by often ostentatious ear spools, nose pieces and pectorals – many made from metal alloys that were easily worked by hammering, casting and gilding to achieve desirable reflective surfaces. Additional apparel included other kinds of headgear, wristlets, belts and arm and leg

Ceramic portrait vessel of a Moche lord (p. 103).

Moche, Peru, 2nd–8th century AD. Ht 33 cm.
The term 'stirrup-spout' has been widely used to describe the distinctive form on top of the most prestigious Moche vessels – an unfortunate misnomer, bestowed by early collectors, arising from its superficial similarity with the shape of a horse stirrup. In fact the conjoined spout encapsulates deep-rooted and pervasive Andean beliefs about the significance of opposing forces joining to become one, and its origins pre-date Moche culture by at least a thousand years (see pp. 78–9, 84).

bands, all of which might have pendant dangles and bells attached.

A seat or stool was usually a ruler's treasured personal possession. These stools range from a Taíno chief's *duho* set with gold and shell inlay to the Inca king's *tiana* upon which he sat, raised on a stepped dais, to perform certain public duties and functions. So placed, the Inca king embodied the idea of an intermediary linking the underworld, earthly and celestial realms. A carefully ordered hierarchy of seats in different materials was the principal means of assigning rank and status in the Andes.

Ruling lords were responsible for overseeing the general prosperity and well-being of their subjects and were charged with the task of maintaining cosmic balance and order. They were required to preside over the seasonal festivals that marked the critical times for planting and harvesting within the agricultural cycle (see pp. 86–7). This might entail an annual round of astronomical observations to announce the beginning of the year as well as ritual pilgrimages along prescribed routes to sacred places in the landscape. If this cosmic order went awry, the ruler could be held personally liable, as in the case of one Chimú ruler who suffered calamitous El Niño flooding during his reign. The angry populace is said to have trussed him up and cast him into the sea as an offering in an effort to placate the gods and restore the natural balance. As imperial domains were extended, carefully orchestrated pomp and ceremony helped to incorporate subject peoples and conquered territories. Rulers combined political, religious and military roles to wield power based on claims to divine authority.

This hammered gold disk is likely to have been used as a pendant ear ornament. At the centre is the embossed head of a Manteño lord himself wearing ear ornaments and with a tri-lobed cap bearing a repeated motif of concentric circles (opposite).

Around the circumference runs a border of smaller panels enclosing either a bat with curling snout and outstretched wings or the head of another creature with pairs of curling volutes. Both allude to the hidden powers of the night-time realm and the underworld.

Embossed gold disk.
Manteño, Ecuador,
9th–15th century AD.
Diam. 10 cm.

Ear spool. Shell and stone mosaic on wood. Chimú, Peru, 12th–15th century AD. Diam. 10 cm.

The frontal standing figure portrayed on this ear spool is an accurate representation of how the wearer would have been attired with a suite of ceremonial regalia proclaiming his divine powers and attributes. A huge fan-shaped headdress was probably composed of a dazzling array of featherwork from different species of tropical birds (see p. 106).

Matching this are ostentatious circular ear spools like these (see pp. 103, 105). He also wears a necklace, shirt and skirt, with tassels hanging from his elbows, and brandishes a large 'staff of office' in either hand. All these details are picked out in inlaid red and purple shell of the thorny oyster (*Spondylus princeps* and *Spondylus calcifer*) and white mother-of-pearl (*Pinctada mazatlanica*) as well as precious stones in a range of greenish hues.

Ceramic portrait vessel of a Moche lord.
Moche, Peru, 2nd–8th century AD. Ht 33 cm.

The finest Moche portrait vessels have long
been renowned for their vivid, naturalistic sense
of individuality (see p. 54). The thin-lipped, hard-
eyed gaze of this figure conveys a commanding
presence (see p. 99). He wears a textile band
with a serrated fringe and panels, each with the
same geometric decoration. From this hangs a
protective back flap extending down over the

neck and back. Small, rounded ear spools are
inserted into a perforation of his lower earlobes.

Considerable numbers of these portrait
vessels were produced and may have served to
project and promote the image of a ruler beyond
his immediate courtly entourage. As tomb
offerings they might carry a convincing likeness
of the owner into the realm of the dead.

Four-cornered hat. Camelid wool.
Wari, Peru, 7th–10th century AD. Ht 9 cm, w. 16 cm.
Andean weavers developed a distinctive form of hat with the corners embellished into tassels or peaks. These have come to be known as 'four-cornered hats' and seem to have been worn as status symbols on ceremonial occasions and to have been buried with their owners at death. The dense designs on this example are composed of columns of vertically stacked faces with appendages, arranged in a strict geometric grid, each square with a different colour and background. The upraised arms of one figure recall the pose of the Andean Staff Deity, whose image is a pervasive presence in Andean art.

Ceramic male portrait vessel.
Tiwanaku, Bolivia, 6th–10th century AD.
Ht 13 cm, w. 9.5 cm.

The accomplished execution of this rare portrait
of a Tiwanaku lord bears comparison with the
better-known Moche portrait vessels (see
pp. 54, 99, 103). He wears a fez-like circular
woven round hat rather than a four-cornered hat
– examples of both have been found preserved
in burials. His ear spools and lip plug are
standard emblems for high-ranking males. The
surface has been assiduously burnished to
achieve a uniform buff-coloured appearance.
The headpiece finished in a dark red slip and a
roughened strip on one side suggests there was
once an appliqué appendage of some kind that
has since broken off.

Featherwork panel.
Peru, 15th–16th century AD. **L. 81 cm, w. 54 cm.**
The brilliantly coloured plumage of tropical birds was highly prized and demanded specialized fabrication techniques and skills. The spectrum of available colours and visual impact of featherwork went beyond what could be achieved with the range of pigments used in dyeing and painting.

This panel is composed of a cotton plain-weave ground cloth covered with overlapping rows of feathers on lengths of cotton yarn running across the textile. At first sight it appears to be the front of a tunic, but it lacks a neck slit. The pendant 'V' and 'waistband' stripe are picked out in rich red and yellow against a blue ground and recall the core design found on many Inca *unkus* (sleeveless tunics). As their empire rapidly expanded in the course of the 15th century, the Incas imposed tribute obligations to satisfy the demand for exotic materials including a great volume of feathers. There is little direct evidence for this in the Andean highlands, but this panel may be an example of provincial Inca featherwork that has survived on the coast.

Tunic of camelid wool and metal dangles.
Tiwanaku-Wari, Peru/Bolivia, 7th–10th century AD.
L. 99 cm, w. 95 cm.

Elite tunics such as this were produced at the great pre-Inca
urban centres of Wari and Tiwanaku, whose territory spanned
much of highland Peru and Bolivia. Their textile arts show a
bold visual vocabulary of abstract motifs that signalled vital
information concerning ethnic identity, lineage, rank and office.
Analysis of the attached circular metal dangles confirms that
the metal is ancient, but that modern thread has been used to
sew them to the tunic. No known precedents exist for this on
textiles of the period and they seem to have been added more
recently, perhaps in order to enhance the appeal and
contemporary value of the piece.

**Chief's stool (*duho*). Wood with gold inlay, Taíno,
Caribbean Islands, 15th–16th century AD. L. 44 cm, ht 22 cm.**

One of the most striking Taíno masterworks is this chief's stool sculpted
from the dense tropical hardwood guayacan (*Guaiacum officinale*). It
assumes the form of a powerful male figure with ear spools crouching on
all fours with his head tilted up and mouth locked open in a tense grimace.
The inscribed patterns just below the shoulders and on the backrest
represent cotton armbands and a waistband. The Taíno prized the
hardness, durability and above all the blackness of the guayacan for their
most precious religious objects (see pp. 26–8). Black represented night and
was also equated with the absence of colour in the invisible spirit realm.
Hammered gold inlay was placed in the eyes to indicate the ability to 'see'
into this supernatural world. Gold was also applied to the joints – the points
of articulation that maintain the component body parts as an integral whole.
Chiefs and shamans used these 'seats of power' to intercede with the
ancestor spirits (*cemís*) and to help manage and control the invisible forces
governing the natural world as well as human affairs (see p. 119).

Ocelot-shaped offering vessel in quartz (*onyx*).
Teotihuacan, Mexico, 150 BC–AD 750.
L. 33.5 cm, ht 16 cm.

This offering vessel represents an ocelot (*Leopardus pardalis*), the largest of a number of highland species of small wild cat that grows up to a metre in length, has a long tail and fur patterned like that of a jaguar. Fashioned from a single block of prestigious white alabaster, it emphasizes the flat surfaces and formal geometric elements found on many Teotihuacan stone funerary masks (see p. 137), imparting a distinctive 'corporate' style to the architecture and sculpture from this site.

**Greenstone belt mould in the form of a toad.
Classic Veracruz, Mexico, 4th–12th century AD.
L. 39.5 cm, ht 12 cm.**

Sculptures like this were once erroneously
interpreted as 'yokes' worn when playing the
Mesoamerican ballgame. In fact they were used as
moulds for shaping the protective leather belts
secured to the waists of players to cushion the
impact of the heavy rubber ball. The ball court itself
was a carefully circumscribed sacred space and a
symbolic entrance to the Underworld for the losers
in what was a life-and-death contest. The toad
lives at the threshold between the earthly and
subterranean worlds. (See pp. 12–13.)

Jadeite ritual perforator.
Olmec, Mexico, 12th–14th century BC.
L. 38 cm.

Ritual bloodletting was an ancient and widespread practice in Mesoamerica. It was undertaken as a solemn sacrificial gesture to deified ancestors in order to maintain a mindful and respectful relationship and elicit their goodwill in return. This kind of reciprocity underlay much of Mesoamerican religious practice. Bloodletting implements were fashioned out of bone, flint, green stones, stingray spines and shark teeth and were used in self-sacrifice rites which involved drawing blood from various parts of the body.

Carved in precious green jadeite, the size of this Olmec perforator suggests that it was not actually used for bloodletting, but instead served as a highly visible element of ritual regalia to be carried and displayed on ceremonial occasions. The cleft glyph at the top recalls those on the Olmec adze and Teotihuacan stone mask (pp. 136–7) and underlines the key symbolic purpose of these ritual instruments, which was to pierce the membrane marking the threshold between the visible and invisible worlds.

Stone lintel showing Lord Shield Jaguar and Lady K'abal Xook bloodletting. Lintel 24, Maya, Yaxchilan, Guatemala, c. AD 725. Ht 109.7 cm, w. 77.3 cm.

Itzamnaaj Bahlam II (Lord Shield Jaguar) acceded to the throne at Yaxchilan in October AD 681 and commissioned a series of magnificent buildings. Lady K'abal Xook, his most prominent wife, initiated three extraordinary sculptures for the front doorways of structure 23: lintels 24, 25 and 26. These works mark a remarkable era of artistic and political vigour for the city. The lintels were commissioned between AD 723 and 726, when the building was formally dedicated by 'entering with fire'. The scene on Lintel 24 depicts Lord Shield Jaguar and Lady K'abal Xook engaged in a bloodletting rite that took place on 9.13.17.15.12 5 *eb* 15 *mac* in the Maya calendar (28 October AD 709). She kneels in front of Shield Jaguar who holds a great torch described in the text as a 'burning spear', illuminating a ritual that was probably held at night or set in the dark recess of a private chamber. Both king and queen are richly attired with Sun God pectorals. The human head worn by Shield Jaguar over his brow may be a shrunken battle trophy. Wearing an exquisitely woven *huipil*, Lady K'abal Xook pulls a thorned rope through her tongue in the principal form of blood sacrifice performed by royal women. The rope falls on to an open codex.

**Ceramic painted vessel ('The Fenton Vase').
Maya, Nebaj, Guatemala, 7th–8th century AD.
Diam. 16 cm.**

Maya polychrome painted vases bear scenes
rich in observed detail, which are combined with
glyphic texts that communicate information
about the names of the main protagonists, the
dates when key events took place and the
nature and purpose of the exchange. This
renowned vase records an interaction that is
probably taking place in a palace setting.

From the left in the rollout scene a kneeling
visitor presents a delivery of tribute consisting
of a basket piled high with *tamales* (maize
cakes). In the centre of the scene a ruler seated
on a raised platform leans forward to receive the
gift. Behind him a seated scribe is busy noting
details of the exchange.

**Jadeite plaque of seated king and dwarf.
Maya, 7th–9th century AD. Ht 14 cm, w. 14 cm.**
This Maya king is depicted cross-legged atop a
raised dais with regal regalia including a plumed
headdress, ear spools, bar pectoral and a royal
belt. The war shield on his left arm bears the
image of the Jaguar god of the underworld.
His speech scroll suggests the declaration of a
formal edict. Below stands an attendant dwarf,
part of the royal entourage. This plaque was
found at Teotihuacan, apparently taken there
from one of the Classic Maya cities.

7

Entering the Spirit World

One of the threads running through this book is the relationship between an invisible world – the timeless and ever-present spirit realm – and the visible world, where the creative forces that drive the universe find material expression in space and time. When Taíno shamans asked the *cemí* spirit within a tree to identify itself before they began sculpting, the resulting form might be a bird, turtle, human or a composite blend of anthropomorphic and zoomorphic attributes (see ch. 2). These beings were all active agents in a dynamic universe of constantly changing forms and

Sandstone sculpture of the female deity Tlazolteotl. Huaxtec, Mexico, 10th–15th century AD. Ht 150 cm, w. 50 cm. Sculptures from Mexico's northern Gulf Coast depict Tlazolteotl, a goddess associated with spinning, weaving, childbirth and curing. As the 'eater of filth' she was responsible for absorbing and absolving the guilt of sinful deeds. Her spectacular fan-shaped headdress would originally have been made from beaten bark cloth and brightly painted. A single large but rather thin slab of sandstone was used to sculpt this figure, imposing constraints on its depth and volume.

appearances. Some of the figures represent humans in a state of ecstatic possession – their exposed skeletal ribs and vertebrae indicate that they exist between the worlds of the living and the dead. Other objects that serve specific practical purposes and functions are imbued with a palpable animate energy. Those such as snuff trays, used to effect altered states of consciousness, bear dense, repetitive patterns in which the boundary between material and immaterial worlds begins to dissolve (see p. 118). Yet other works, such as the prismatic sculptures of Tlazolteotl (goddess of childbirth and weaving), have skulls carved on their backs – they stand at the threshold between life and death, Janus-like, looking into both worlds.

The ancestral realm is intimately connected with underworld powers that are the sources of earthly fertility and burgeoning life. Designated sacred spaces were built into the fabric of emerging towns and cities and provided the settings where these other-worldly connections were consummated and celebrated. They range from the semi-subterranean *kivas* (sweat baths) of the southwestern USA to the sunken courtyards of Chavín de Huantar and Tiwanaku. The Inca used a special central place known as the *ushnu*, marked by a tiered platform, to toast the sun. Libations were poured into the body of the earth through a nearby vertical shaft. Public avenues and the facades of major buildings were often aligned towards key points on the horizon that were associated with regular solar and lunar movements.

Pyramids were built skyward and often supported temple structures which restricted access to all but a select few. These man-made mountains were the dominating architectural stage and backdrop for ritual theatre. Recent investigations have revealed that one such construction in Teotihuacan, the Pyramid of the Sun, was built atop womb-like passages and caves concealed in an ancient lava flow below. In the Maya city of Palenque the tomb of Lord Pakal, who ruled in the 8th century AD, is embedded deep within a structure commissioned by the ruler himself while he was still alive and dedicated to him upon his death. This pattern is repeated at Tikal, Monte Albán and numerous similar sites where the dead were buried with personal possessions and other offerings to accompany, comfort and console them on their journey into the spirit realm.

Wooden anaconda snuff tray.
Brazil, 19th–early 20th century AD. **L. 35 cm.**
Imagery connected with altered states of
consciousness is found on the ritual
paraphernalia associated with the preparation
and consumption of hallucinogenic snuff. The
circular central depression on to which the snuff
was placed is enclosed by serpentine designs.
The handle is in the form of an anaconda, a
large and much feared constrictor that first
crushes its prey then swallows it whole,
including occasional unwary humans. The
object was held so that the user was faced
with the re-curved head of the serpent. The
shamans who ingested the snuff were said to
journey back into the body of the ancestral
anaconda.

Wooden stool (*duho*).
Taíno, Hispaniola (Dominican Republic), 15th–16th century AD.
L. 72.5 cm, w. 30 cm.

The consequences of inhaling hallucinogenic snuff are explicitly represented in this crouching male *cemí* (spirit being). The unusual view of the underside reveals the skeletal ribcage and prominent sexual organ that embodies the potent masculinity of a founding male ancestor. His toes are tightly bunched and he holds his clenched fists clasped to his face in a rigid, contorted posture typical of someone in the grip of a powerful hallucinatory trance. The exaggerated calf muscles shown on this and other male sculptures (see pp. 27–8) were produced by tightly bound ligatures designed to enhance their hardness and visibility. The elongated head is also the result of binding to achieve aesthetic ideals (see pp. 37–8). The object was carefully shaped to serve as a low stool or perhaps doubled as a neck-rest. (See pp. 108–9.)

Gold alloy lime container.
Quimbaya, Colombia, 7th–11th century AD.
Ht 16.2 cm, diam. 8.6 cm.

This work blends mastery of technique with sensuous elegance to stunning effect. It served as the neck of a lime flask and the four holes around the base were probably used to attach it to a gourd vessel. The two components assembled (metal neck and gourd vessel) would have completed the lime flask. At the top is an encircling row of six human faces, each with an incised line running vertically from the forehead across the eyes and down the cheeks. The closed eyes suggest an inner contemplative concern with the spirit realm, as opposed to the outwardly visible world. Some clues to understanding this state of consciousness are found on lime containers featuring full human figures evidently engaged in solemn seasonal rituals. (See also pp. 82–3.)

Opposite: **Gold mask.**
Quimbaya, Colombia, 7th–11th century AD.
Ht 10.5 cm, w. 12.1 cm.

The closed eyes on this mask, like those on the lime flask, signal a focus on the inner world. The pendant dangles and nose ornament indicate high status. Much smaller than life size and lacking eye perforations, like other similar objects it was probably not intended actually to be worn as a mask. It may have formed part of a suite of carefully guarded treasured heirlooms, only displayed in the course of elaborate ceremonial events.

Wooden bowl with two jaguars.

Brazil, 19th century AD. Ht 10.5 cm, w. 20 cm.

Examples of early wooden sculptures from the Amazon lowlands are extremely rare. Unless guarded and protected, all organic materials quickly succumb to the humid climate and ravages of insects, so very few wooden pieces large or small have survived. The inscribed motifs on this bowl show a fluid rhythmic symmetry that is paralleled in the dense, interlocking designs painted on the pottery of many Amazonian traditions. Inlaid shell was used to highlight the eyes, nose and fanged teeth of a jaguar. The vessel may once have held a hallucinogenic infusion of *ayahuasca* made with the vine *banisteriopsis caapi*. This potent brew would transport the participant into the 'realm of the jaguar' where shamans are accompanied by a spirit companion or may themselves be possessed by a jaguar alter ego. (See pp. 46, 88.)

Carved and painted wooden chest.
Haida or Northwest Coast peoples, British Columbia,
Canada, *c*. AD 1850. L. 29 cm, ht 28 cm, w. 41 cm.
The central frontal figure on this chest is a squatting bear
with upraised front paws flanked by a symmetrical pair of
inward-facing bear heads in profile. Nested beneath his
toothed mouth and between his limbs is a smaller, human
figure who adopts the same posture (see p. 23). The chest
was used for storing ceremonial paraphernalia for periodic
community feasting events known as the *potlatch*.

The images adorning houses, poles, canoes and boxes
are inspired by stories of encounters between ancestors and
animals. Haida legends tell of a princess married to a young
man who turned out to be a bear. She gave birth to bear
people and so the bear became the supporting spirit and
crest of the clan.

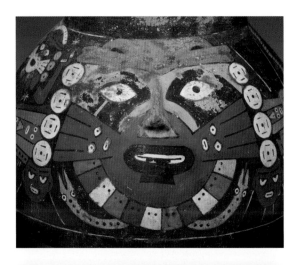

Ceramic jar with masked deity and snakes.

Nasca, Peru, 2nd century BC–6th century AD. Ht 26.5 cm, diam. 22 cm.

The face of an imposing masked deity is painted on the front of this large globular urn. Like the deity on the vessel on p. 127, he wears a mouth-mask (but of a different style) as well as a diadem on his forehead. Actual gold mouth-masks and diadems have been found in tombs and suggest that deity impersonators wore ritual attire adorned with these kinds of objects, perhaps as participants in ritual re-enactments of significant creation events. This figure also wears a necklace of rectangular plaques of different colours, each with a pair of perforations used to string them together. These also find their counterpart in archaeological finds fashioned from the red shell of the thorny oyster (*Spondylus princeps*). It is possible that the two sets of four circular white elements arranged vertically on either side of the face were also shell ornaments, perhaps mother of pearl (*Pinctada mazatlanica*). A severed head hangs beneath each. The deity's extended right hand holds a small figure by the waist, similarly attired and brandishing an *atlatl* (spear-thrower), who may represent a revered ancestor. In his extended left hand the deity grasps a severed head whose mouth has been sealed by inserting a pair of long *huarango* thorns. The hair of the deity is composed of a lively gorgon-like tangle of snakes. These snakes have pairs of small 'legs' which, according to people living in the area today, helps explain how snakes 'run so fast'.

Dyed cotton textile fragment.
Paracas, South Coast Peru,
7th century BC–1st century AD. L. 57 cm, w. 12 cm.
Embroidered Paracas textiles feature a wide array of animals and plants of the desert coast. Here, a small creature with a striped pattern on its back lies above the head and body of a larger animal facing in the same direction. The latter has a broad mouth with rows of teeth, upturned eyes, two pairs of limbs, and a serrated motif on either side of its body. These traits suggest that it may be a reptile, perhaps a large land lizard, and its elongated tail is entwined with the tail of another with different body markings rendered in different colours.

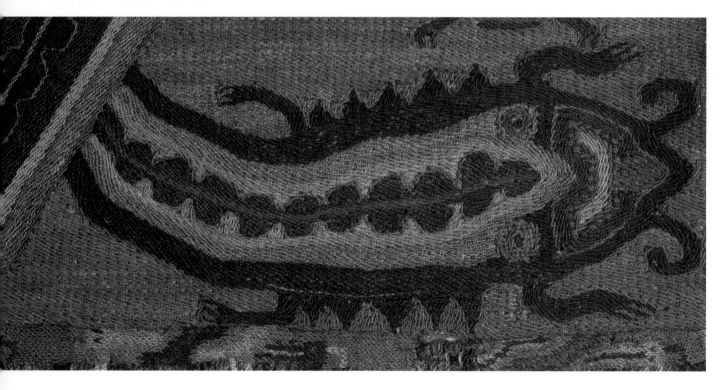

**Double-spout and bridge ceramic jar
with puma deity.**
**Nasca, Peru, 2nd century BC–6th century AD.
Ht 32 cm.**

The striking polychrome imagery on this vessel features a being with large round eyes which wears a feline mouth-mask with long whiskers ending in volutes that identify him as the puma deity. Affixed to his forehead is a distinctive diadem with a schematized frontal face in the middle. He grasps an inverted severed human head in his paws flanked by two down-turned hanks of hair trimmed straight across at the ends. The sprinkling of red dots applied between the eyes and mouth on the head represent spots of blood. Likewise the pupils of the eyes are only half visible, a convention widely used in Andean art which alludes to the way the eyes of a dying person roll upwards at the threshold between life and death. The protruding tongue that extends from the mouth of the deity to that of the severed head establishes a dynamic connection between the world of the living and the world of the dead (see also p. 125).

The deity is wearing a cloak or cape emblazoned with bold zigzag motifs in alternating colours which extend on to the tail plume visible at the back. A pair of bird talons hangs limply beneath. This avian attire may signal that the puma deity is bearing the severed head away on a celestial journey. Beneath the black line that marks an inflection in the vessel wall, the lower third bears a row of crescent-shaped motifs.

Gold *capacocha* figurines.
Inca, 14th–15th century AD. Ht *c.* 6 cm.
Miniature figurines wrought in hammered gold were deposited as offerings to accompany high-altitude human sacrifices made in the course of the Inca state ritual of *capacocha*, meaning royal sin or obligation. These events took place upon the death of an Inca king and were used to incorporate new territory into the rapidly expanding Inca empire.

The local lords of subject ethnic groups were required to select and send to Cusco unblemished children embodying the ideal of human perfection. Here the young children were

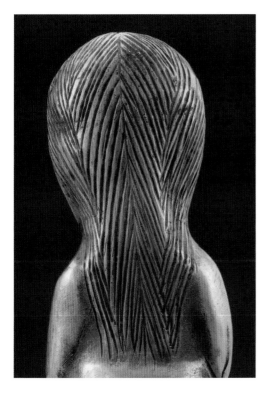

ritually married and presented with sets of miniature human and llama figurines in gold, silver, copper and shell. The male figures have elongated earlobes and a braided headband (*llauto*), while the female figures wear long plaited tresses in different styles. Both male and female figures hold their hands clasped to their chests in a gesture of supplication or reverence. The children along with their offerings were then returned to their original communities, where they were feted and honoured before being sacrificed to the mountain deities (*apus*). (See p. 72.)

The face of the warrior peers out from the open beak of the eagle headdress. The design is picked out in tiny tesserae made from turquoise and malachite together with four different species of shell: red *Spondylus princeps* (thorny oyster), white *Strombus galeatus* (conch), pink *Strombus gigas* (queen conch) and iridescent *Pinctada mazatlanica* (mother of pearl).

Ceremonial flint knife with wood and mosaic handle. Aztec-Mixtec, Mexico, AD 1300–1521. L. 31.7 cm, ht 9 cm.

This is a rare example of a ceremonial knife where the flint blade and its wooden handle have both survived. Many plain flint blades have been found in the caches of dedicated offerings excavated in and around the Templo Mayor, the principal temple in the heart of the Aztec capital Tenochtitlan. These blades are sometimes embedded in a block of copal resin so as to stand vertically, thus representing the glyph *tecpatl* meaning 'flint' or 'sacrificial' knife. This glyph is associated with one of the 'year bearers' in the 260-day Aztec calendar (*tonalpohualli*) and with cardinal north, the direction of death and cold.

The handle of this knife is fashioned in cedar wood (*cedrela odorata*) in the form of a crouching eagle warrior (see pp. 50, 59), one of two warrior orders, the other being jaguar, that served the ruling lord (*tlatoani*). Radiography reveals that the hafting is too shallow for the knife to have been functionally effective, which suggests that it was used for symbolic ceremonial purposes.

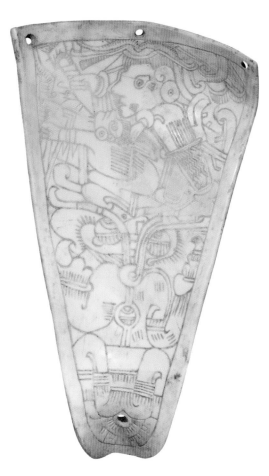

Carved shell pendant.

Huaxtec, Mexico, 10th–15th century AD.

Ht 16 cm, w. 9.5 cm.

This pendant was fashioned from a section of conch shell and worn suspended from the neck. The inscribed scene depicts in profile a priest grasping with his left hand the hair of a smaller kneeling figure in front, thereby forcing his head upwards. In his right hand he wields a large blade pointed at the throat of the sacrificial victim (see p. 130). The resulting flow of blood will stream down into the open, upturned jaws of the earth deity squatting below with upraised clawed hands. Blood sacrifice was offered to nourish the earth and to assure the growth of crops needed to sustain human life.

Stone offering vessel (*cuauhxicalli*).
Aztec, Mexico, AD 1300–1521.
Ht 56 cm, diam. 30 cm.

Chroniclers' accounts from around the time of the Spanish conquest of Mexico in the early 16th century record that *cuauhxicalli* (eagle vessels) served as receptacles for sacrificial offerings. One renowned example in the form of an eagle from the Templo Mayor, the principal temple in the heart of the Aztec capital Tenochtitlan, was sculpted from basalt and weighs nearly two tons. These kinds of objects were probably used in the solemn state ceremonies of investiture and enthronement of new kings.

The shape of this vessel echoes that of pottery containers used for storing *pulque*. The upper part comprises encircling superimposed bands of motifs representing human hearts, feathers and jade. The front bears a solar disk and the glyph 4 Movement, the symbol for the fifth epoch in the Aztec creation cycle. On the base beneath this is the glyph 1 Rain. On the obverse side is a symbol for the moon together with the glyph 2 Rabbit, one of the calendrical names for the *pulque* god. The sun-moon opposition expresses a persistent Mesoamerican concern with opposed, complementary forces governing the relationship between natural events and human affairs.

The vessel shows signs of having been intentionally defaced, especially at the sides where there is extensive damage. The hollow basin at the top and some details of the exterior surface were never completed. This suggests that an unexpected event, perhaps the arrival of the Spanish, intervened before the piece could be finished.

Sandstone sculpture of Mictlantecuhtli.
Aztec, Mexico, AD 1400–1521. Ht 60 cm, w. 27 cm.
This figure is sculpted from sandstone, which is not found in the Mexican highlands and was probably quarried and transported from a source on Mexico's northern Gulf Coast. It bears three inscribed glyphs: Four House is carved on the lower back, Two Skull appears on the carefully combed hair, and Five Vulture is visible on the right shoulder. The skeletal facial features represent Mictlantecuhtli, a minor Aztec deity and denizen of the Underworld (Mictlan), where he occupied the lowest of the nine levels into which it was divided.

The souls of the deceased were destined for a specific level in Mictlan according to the circumstances of their death. Those who died of natural causes could attain the ninth level but had to negotiate many obstacles to reach it. Two remarkable large ceramic sculptures of Mictlantecuhtli were recovered in the course of excavations undertaken in the 1980s in the House of the Eagles at the Templo Mayor, the religious centre of the Aztec capital Tenochtitlan. These bore traces of blood consistent with depictions in the codices (screenfold books) of ceremonies in which an image of Mictlantecuhtli, or a person representing him, is bathed with blood.

Votive jade axe.

Olmec, Mexico, 12th–4th century BC. Ht 28 cm.

This massive ceremonial axe (*celt*) combines characteristics of the caiman and the jaguar, the most powerful predators inhabiting the rivers and forests of the tropical lowlands. The pronounced cleft in the head mimics the indentation found on the skulls of jaguars and has been compared to the human fontanelle. These clefts feature on other Olmec sculptures and in imagery in which vegetal motifs spring from similar cracks and orifices, alluding to the underground sources of fertility and life. The crossed bands glyph lightly incised on the waistband represents an entrance or opening and is repeated on a jade perforator (p. 112).

This combination of symbols on the axe proclaims its magical power to cleave open the portals to the underworld, reinforcing the association of *celts* with agriculture and maize – ground stone axes were indispensable for felling forest trees and clearing ground for planting. Utilitarian objects were often personified in this way so as to represent the qualities and attributes of supernatural deities. Accumulating inner soul force, they became potent objects that were handed down from one generation to the next.

Opposite: **Greenstone mask.**

Teotihuacan, Mexico, 1st–8th century AD.

Ht 24 cm, w. 26 cm.

Masks like this were sculpted in materials carefully selected for their visual qualities and symbolic value. The eyes and mouth would originally have been inlaid with shell. They are sometimes described as funerary masks or may perhaps have been mounted on a wooden armature and dressed with elaborate costumes to embody deified ancestors and gods. The cleft incision in the top of this mask is reminiscent of the cleft in the head of the votive jade axe (left), hinting at widespread underlying continuities in Mesoamerican belief and symbolism.

8

Further Information

FURTHER READING

Ancient America: General works
Anton, F. & Dockstader, F. J. (eds), *Pre-Columbian Art and Later Indian Tribal Arts*, Abrams, 1968
Coe, M. D., Snow, D. & Benson, E., *Atlas of Ancient America*, Facts on File, 1986
Dockstader, F. J., *Indian Art in America: Arts and Crafts*, New York Graphic Society, 1961
Easby, E. K. (ed.), *Before Cortés: Sculpture of Middle America*, Metropolitan Museum of Art, 1970
Kubler, G., *The Art and Architecture of Ancient America*, Yale University Press, 1992
Levenson, J. A. (ed.), *Circa 1492: Art in the Age of Exploration*, National Gallery of Art, 1991
Pasztory, E. *Pre-Columbian Art*, Cambridge University Press, 1998
Townsend, R. (ed.), *The Ancient Americas: Art from Sacred Landscapes*, Art Institute of Chicago, 1992

North America

General works
Berlo, J. C. & Phillips, R. B., *Native North American Art*, Oxford University Press, 1998
Feest, C. F., *Native Arts of North America*, Thames and Hudson, 1992
King, J. C. H., *First Peoples First Contacts*, British Museum Press, 1999
Penney, D. & Horse Capture, G., *North American Indian Art*, Thames and Hudson, 2004
Sturtevant, W. C. (ed.), *Handbook of the North American Indian*, Smithsonian Institution Press, 1990

North
Fitzhugh, W. H. & Crowell, A., *Crossroads of Continents: Cultures of Siberia and Alaska*, Smithsonian Institution Press, 1988
King, J. C. H. & Feest, C. F. (eds), *Three Centuries of Woodlands Indian Art*, ZVF Publishers, 2007

South
Cordell, L., *Ancient Pueblo Peoples*, St Remy Press, 1994
Plog, S., *Peoples of the Ancient Southwest*, Thames and Hudson, 1997
Townsend, R. F. (ed.), *Casas Grandes and the Ceramic Art of the Ancient Southwest*, Yale University Press, 2005
Townsend, R. F. & Sharp, R. V. (eds), *Hero, Hawk and Open Hand: American Indian Art of the Ancient Midwest and South*, Art Institute of Chicago/Yale University Press, 2004

Mesoamerica

General works
Coe, M. D., *Mexico: From the Olmecs to the Aztecs*, Thames and Hudson, 2008
Hendon, J. & Joyce, R. (eds) *Mesoamerican Archaeology*, Blackwell, 2004
Miller, M. E., *The Art of Mesoamerica: From Olmec to Aztec*, Thames and Hudson, 4th edn, 2006
Solis, F., *National Museum of Anthropology: Mexico City*, Abrams, 2004
Evans, S. T., *Ancient Mexico and Central America*, Thames and Hudson, 2008
Evans, S. T. & Webster, D. L. (eds), *Archaeology of Ancient Mexico and Central America: An Encyclopedia*, Routledge, 2000

Aztecs
McEwan, C., Middleton, A., Cartwright, C. & Stacey, R., *Turquoise Mosaics from Mexico*, British Museum Press, 2006
Moctezuma, E.M. & Olguín, F. S., *Aztecs*, Royal Academy of Arts, 2002
Pasztory, E., *Aztec Art*, University of Oklahoma Press, 2000
Solis, F., *The Aztec Empire*, Guggenheim Museum Publications, 2004
Townsend, R.F., *The Aztecs*, Thames and Hudson, 2000

Caribbean
Bercht, F., Brodsky, E., Farmer, J. & Taylor, D. (eds), *Taíno: Pre-Columbian Art and Culture from the Caribbean*, Monacelli Press, 1997
Oliver, J., McEwan, C. & Casas Gilberga, A. (eds), *El Caribe Precolombino*, Museu Barbier-Mueller d'Art Precolombí, 2008
Oliver, J. R., *Caciques and Cemí Idols: The Web Spun by Taíno Rulers between Hispaniola and Puerto Rico*, University of Alabama Press, forthcoming 2009

Maya
Coe, M. D., *The Maya*, Thames and Hudson, 2005
Demarest, A., *Ancient Maya: Rise and Fall of a Rainforest Civilization*, Cambridge University Press, 2004
Fields, V.M. & Reents-Budet, D. (eds), *Lords of Creation: The Origins of Sacred Maya Kingship*, Scala, 2005
Martin, S. & Grube, N., *Chronicle of the Maya Kings and Queens*, Thames and Hudson, 2008
Miller, M., *Maya Art and Architecture*, Thames and Hudson, 2000
Miller, M. & Martin, S., *Courtly Art of the Ancient Maya*, Thames and Hudson, 2004
Miller, M. & Taube, K., *An Illustrated Dictionary of the Gods and Symbols of Ancient Mexico and the Maya*, Thames and Hudson, 1997
Schele, L. & Mathews, P., *The Code of Kings: The Language of Seven Sacred Maya Temples and Tombs*, Scribner, 1998
Sharer, R. with Traxler, L. P., *The Ancient Maya*, Stanford University Press, 2005
Tedlock, D., *Popol Vuh: The Definitive Edition of the Mayan Book of the Dawn of Life*, Touchstone, 1996

Mexico: North/West
Fields, V. M. & Zamudio-Taylor, V., *The Road to Aztlan: Art from a Mythic Homeland*, Los Angeles County Museum of Art, 2001
Townsend, R. F., *Ancient West Mexico*, Thames and Hudson, 1998

Olmecs

Benson, E. & de la Fuente, B. (eds), *Olmec Art of Ancient Mexico*, National Gallery of Art, Washington, DC, 1996

Clark, J. & Pye, M. (eds), *Olmec Art and Archaeology in Mesoamerica*, Yale University Press, 2006

Coe, M. D., *The Olmec World: Ritual and Rulership*, Princeton University Art Museum/Abrams, 1996

Diehl, R., *The Olmecs: America's First Civilization*, Thames and Hudson, 2004

Teotihuacan

Berlo, J. (ed.), *Art, Ideology, and the City of Teotihuacan*, Dumbarton Oaks, 1992

Berrin, K. & Pasztory, E., *Teotihuacan: Art from the City of the Gods*, Thames and Hudson, 1994

Zapotecs

Marcus, J. & Kent V, F., *Zapotec Civilization: How Urban Society Evolved in Mexico's Oaxaca Valley*, Thames and Hudson, 1996

Codices

Boone, E., *Stories in Red and Black: Pictorial Histories of the Aztecs and Mixtecs*, University of Texas Press, 2008

Brotherston, G., *Painted Books from Mexico*, British Museum Press, 1995

Gruzinski, S., *Painting the Conquest*, Flammarion, 1992

South America

General works

Berrin, K. (ed.), *The Spirit of Ancient Peru: Treasures from the Museo Arqueologico Rafael Larco-Herrera*, Thames and Hudson, 1997

Burger, R., *Chavín and the Origins of Peruvian Civilization*, Thames and Hudson, 1992

Lumbreras, L.G., *Peru: Art from the Chavín to the Incas*, Skira, 2006

Morris, C., Von Hagen, A. (eds), *The Inca Empire and its Andean Origins*, American Museum of Natural History/Abbeville Press, 1993

Moseley, M. E., *The Incas and their Ancestors: The Archaeology of Peru*, Thames and Hudson, 2001

Quilter, J., *Treasures of the Andes: The Glories of Inca and Pre-Columbian South America*, Duncan Baird, 2006

Reid, J. W., *Magic Feathers: Textile Art from Ancient Peru*, Textile and Art Publications, 2005

Silverman, H. & Isbell, W. (eds), *Handbook of South American Archaeology*, Springer, 2008

Stone-Miller, R., *Art of the Andes: From Chavín to Inca*, Thames and Hudson, 2002

Inca

D'Altroy, T., *The Incas*, Blackwell, 2002

McEwan, G. F., *The Incas: New Perspectives*, Norton, 2008

Urton, G., *Signs of the Inka Khipu: Binary Coding in the Andean Knotted-String Records*, University of Texas Press, 2003

Urton, G., *Inca Myths*, British Museum Press, 1999

Moche

Bawden, G., *The Moche: Peoples of America*, Blackwell, 1999

Benson, E., *The Mochica*, Thames and Hudson, 1972

Bourget, S. & Jones, K. L., *The Art and Archaeology of the Moche: An Ancient Andean Society of the Peruvian North Coast*, University of Texas Press, forthcoming 2009

Bourget, S., *Sex, Death and Sacrifice in Moche Religion and Visual Culture*, University of Texas Press, 2006

Donnan, C. B., *Ceramics of Ancient Peru*, UCLA, 1993

Donnan, C. B., *Moche Tombs at Dos Cabezas: Cotsen*, UCLA, 2007

Donnan, C. B. & McClelland, D., *Moche Fineline Painting: Its Evolution and its Artists*, UCLA, 1999

Pillsbury, J., *Moche Art and Archaeology in Ancient Peru*, National Gallery of Art, Washington, DC, 2006

Nasca

Aveni, A. F., *Nasca: Eighth Wonder of the World?* British Museum Press, 2000

Kroeber, A. & Collier, D., *The Archaeology and Pottery of Nazca Peru: Alfred Kroeber's 1926 Expedition*, Alta Mira Press, 1999

Proulx, D. A., *A Sourcebook of Nasca Ceramic Iconography: Reading a Culture through its Art*, University of Iowa Press, 2006

Silverman, H., *Cahuachi in the Ancient Nasca World*, University of Iowa Press, 1993

Silverman, H. & Proulx, D., *The Nasca*, Blackwell, 2002

Paracas

Paul, A. (ed.), *Paracas Art and Architecture: Objects and Context in South Coastal Peru*, University of Iowa Press, 1991

Wari & Tiwanaku

Janusek, J., *Ancient Tiwanaku*, Cambridge University Press, 2007

Kolata, A., *The Tiwanaku: Portrait of an Andean Civilization*, Blackwell, 1993

McEwan, G. F., *Pikillacta: The Wari Empire in Cuzco*, University of Iowa Press, 2005

Stanish, M. C., *Ancient Titicaca*, University of California Press, 2003

Young-Sanchez, M. (ed.), *Tiwanaku: Ancestors of the Inca*, University of Nebraska Press, 2004

Amazon

McEwan, C., Barreto, C. & Neves, E., *Unknown Amazon*, British Museum Press, 2001

Colombia

Labbé, A. (ed.), *Shamans, Gods, and Mythic Beasts: Colombian Gold and Ceramics in Antiquity*, American Federations of Arts, 1998

Labbé, A., *Colombia before Columbus: The People, Culture and Ceramic Art of Prehispanic Colombia*, Rizzoli, 1986

Ecuador

Klein, D. & Cruz Cevallos, I. (eds), *Ecuador: The Secret Art of Precolumbian Ecuador*, Five Continents Editions, 2007

Patagonia

McEwan, C., Borrero, L. A. & Prieto, A. (eds), *Patagonia: Natural History, Prehistory and Ethnography at the Uttermost End of the Earth*, Princeton University Press, 1998

Colonial-period art

Phipps, E., Hecht, J. & Esteras Martín, C., *The Colonial Andes: Tapestries and Silverwork 1530–1830*, Metropolitan Museum of Art/Yale University Press, 2004

Online resources

Foundation for the Advancement of Mesoamerican Studies, Inc.: www.famsi.org/mayawriting/codices/index.html www.worldtimelines.org.uk/world/americas

Collections of Ancient American art

United Kingdom

Museum of Archaeology and Anthropology,
    Cambridge
    www.maa.cam.ac.uk
Pitt-Rivers Museum, Oxford
    www.prm.ox.ac.uk
World Museum, Liverpool
    www.liverpoolmuseums.org.uk/wml
British Museum, London
    www.britishmuseum.org

Europe

Austria:
Museum für Völkerkunde, Vienna
    www.ethno-museum.ac.at

Belgium:
Musées Royaux d'Art et d'Histoire, Brussels
    www.kmkg-mrah.be

France:
Musée du Quai Branly, Paris
    www.quaibranly.fr/en

Germany:
Ethnologisches Museum: Dahlem Museum,
    Staatliche Museen zu Berlin
Staatliches Museum für Völkerkunde München
    www.voelkerkundemuseum-muenchen.de
Linden Museum, Stuttgart
    www.lindenmuseum.de

Netherlands:
Museum Volkenkunde, Leiden
    www.rmv.nl

Sweden:
Museum of World Culture (Varldskulturmuseet),
    Gothenburg
    www.varldskulturmuseet.se

Switzerland:
Museum der Kulturen, Basel
    www.mkb.ch
Museum Rietberg, Zürich
    www.rietberg.ch

Americas

Argentina:
Museo Etnografico Juan B. Ambrosetti, Buenos
    Aires
    www.museoetnografico.filo.uba.ar
Museo de Arqueología de Alta Montaña, Salta
    www.maam.org.ar

Bolivia:
Museo Nacional de Arqueología, La Paz
    www.bolivian.com/arqueologia

Brazil:
Museu Nacional, Rio de Janeiro

Chile:
Museo de Arte Precolombino, Santiago de Chile
    www.precolombino.cl

Colombia:
El Museo del Oro, Bogotá
    www.banrep.gov.co/museo/esp/home.htm

Costa Rica:
Museo Nacional de Costa Rica, San José
    www.museosdecostarica.com
Museo de Oro Precolombino, San José
    www.museosdelbancocentral.org

Guatemala:
Museo Nacional de Arqueología y Etnología,
    Guatemala City
    www.munae.gob.gt

Mexico:
Museo Nacional de Antropología, Mexico City
    www.mna.inah.gob.mx
Museo del Templo Mayor, Mexico City
    www.templomayor.inah.gob.mx
Museo Amparo, Puebla
    www.museoamparo.com
Museo de Antropología de Xalapa, Veracruz
    www.uv.mx/max

Peru:
Museo de Arte Precolombino, Cusco
    www.map.org.pe
Museo Amano, Lima
    www.museoamano.org

Museo Arqueológico Rafael Larco Herrera, Lima
    www.museolarco.org
Museo Nacional de Antropología, Arqueología e
    Historia, Lima
    www.museonacional.perucultural.org.pe
Museo de Oro del Peru, Lima
    www.museoroperu.com.pe
Museo Tumbas Reales, Sipán
    www.tumbasreales.org

Puerto Rico:
Museo de Historia, Antropología y Arte, San
    Juan
    humanidades.uprrp.edu/museo/index.htm
Museo de Historia, Antropología y Arte,
    Universidad de Puerto Rico, Río Piedras
    www.universia.pr/culturaindigena/index_ing.jsp

USA:
Museum of Fine Arts, Boston
    www.mfa.org
Peabody Museum of Archaeology and
    Ethnology, Cambridge, MA
    www.peabody.harvard.edu
The Art Institute of Chicago
    www.artic.edu
The Field Museum, Chicago
    www.fieldmuseum.org
Cleveland Museum of Art, Ohio
    www.clemusart.com
Denver Art Museum, Colorado
    www.denverartmuseum.org
American Museum of Natural History, New York
    www.amnh.org
Brooklyn Museum of Art, New York
    www.brooklynmuseum.org
Metropolitan Museum of Art, New York
    www.metmuseum.org
National Museum of the American Indian,
    Smithsonian Institution, New York
    www.nmai.si.edu
Princeton University Art Museum, New Jersey
    www.artmuseum.princeton.edu
Dumbarton Oaks Research Library and
    Collections, Washington, DC
    www.doaks.org

Chronologies

Regions and dates for peoples and civilizations featured in this book are summarized below for quick reference. Some cultural groups still use the same name as their pre-contact forebears, so dates for these are given for individual objects in the text.

NORTH AMERICA

Algonquian (Ontario, eastern Canada)
Eskimo Aleut (Vancouver/Alaska, northwestern USA)
Huron (Ontario, eastern Canada/northeastern USA)
Iroquois (northeastern USA)
Northwest Coast Peoples (Vancouver, western Canada/northwestern USA)

Woodland Period (Mound City, Ohio, USA): 1000 BC–AD 1000
Casas Grandes (southwestern USA/northern Mexico): AD 1200–1450

Colonial period: AD 1550–1776

MESOAMERICA

Olmec (Gulf coast): 1200–400 BC
Nayarit (western Mexico): 300 BC–AD 300
Teotihuacan (central Mexico): 150 BC–AD 750
Veracruz (Gulf coast): AD 300–1200
Zapotec (southern Mexico): AD 400–800
Maya (eastern Mexico, Belize, Guatemala): AD 600–900
Huaxtec (Gulf coast): AD 900–1450
Mixtec (central Mexico): AD 1200–1521
Aztec (central Mexico): AD 1400–1521
Taíno (Caribbean Islands): AD 800–1600

Colonial period: AD 1521–1821

SOUTH AMERICA

Chavín (northern Peru): 900–200 BC
Paracas (Peru, south coast): 700 BC–AD 100
Nasca (Peru, south coast): 200 BC–AD 600
Moche (Peru, north coast): AD 100–800
Tiwanaku (Bolivia): AD 300–1000
Wari (Peru, highlands): AD 500–1000
Chimú (Peru, north coast): AD 900–1400
Inca (Peru, Bolivia): AD 1400–1535

Additional enduring regional traditions featured in this book
Guyana (Atlantic coast)
Patagonia (Argentina)
Quimbaya (Colombia)

Colonial period: AD 1535–1820s

Glossary

atlatl 'spear-thrower' in Nahuatl, a shaft with a spur or groove into which a spear is fitted in order to achieve greater velocity and distance.

camelid Collective species name for the South American vicuña and guanaco (wild), and the llama and alpaca (domesticated). Llamas and alpacas are important beasts of burden in the Andes, as well as providing meat and wool.

cemí Spirit being or 'life force' in Taíno belief, associated with or inhabiting ritual objects to which the Taíno attributed important powers.

ceque Quechua for 'line', a system of ritual pathways and symbolic boundaries lined by shrines, dividing the Inca empire.

chakana Stepped cross motif recurring in cultures throughout the Andes, symbolizing the three tiers of the cosmos: the underworld, this world and the celestial realm.

chicha Fermented maize beer made in South America.

coya (also *qoya*) Wife of the Inca (king), queen of the Incas.

duho Taíno term for a ceremonial seat or stool of hardwood or stone, used by chiefs or shamans.

glyph Symbol, either pictorial or ideographic, or element of a writing system such as the Maya and Aztec.

kero (also *qero* or *quero*) Beaker, usually one of a pair, used in the Andes for ceremonial drinking and feasting.

Nahuatl A native language of Mexico, spoken by the Aztecs.

paccha (also *paqcha*) Inca ritual drinking or pouring vessel.

Popol Vuh Book of creation and other ancestral stories of the Maya including that of the Hero Twins, passed on orally for generations before being written down in the 17th century.

potlatch Extravagant ceremonial feast among some indigenous peoples of the Northwest Pacific coast, at which gifts are distributed by the host.

pulque Alcoholic drink made in Mesoamerica from the juice of the agave cactus.

Quechua A native language of Peru, spoken by the Incas.

Quetzalcoatl 'Feathered serpent', a principal god of the Aztecs also known in several earlier ancient Mesoamerican societies including Olmec and Teotihuacan. Associated with creation stories, life and fertility, he also appears as Ehecatl-Quetzalcoatl, the life-giving aspect of wind that brings rain clouds (*see also* Tlaloc).

Tlaloc Central Mexican (and Aztec) god of rain and water (*see also* Quetzalcoatl)

ushnu Inca sacred central space often marked by a low, tiered platform.

British Museum registration numbers

Index